OLD TESTAMENT GUIDES

General Editor

R.N. Whybray

GENESIS 1-11

Other titles in this series include

THE SECOND ISAIAH
R.N. Whybray

EXODUS
W. Johnstone

1 AND 2 SAMUEL
R.P. Gordon

PSALMS
J. Day

JUDGES
A.D.H. Mayes

MICAH, NAHUM, OBADIAH
R. Mason

DANIEL
P.R. Davies

JOB
J.H. Eaton

AMOS
A.G. Auld

EZRA AND NEHEMIAH
H.G.M. Williamson

HAGGAI, ZECHARIAH, MALACHI
R.J. Coggins

JEREMIAH
R.P. Carroll

ECCLESIASTES
R.N. Whybray

DEUTERONOMY
R.E. Clements

THE SONG OF SONGS
A. Brenner

GENESIS 1-11

J. Rogerson

Published by JSOT Press
for the Society for Old Testament Study

Published by JSOT Press
JSOT Press is an imprint of
Sheffield Academic Press Ltd
The University of Sheffield
343 Fulwood Road
Sheffield S10 3BP
England

Printed on acid-free paper in Great Britain
by Billing & Sons Ltd
Worcester

British Library Cataloguing in Publication Data

Rogerson, John 1935–
    Genesis.
    1. Christianity. Scriptures
    I. Title   II. Series
    222.1106

ISSN 0264-6498
ISBN 1-85075-274-5

CONTENTS

PREFACE

This Guide falls into two main sections, represented respectively by Chapters 2 and 3. Chapter 2 is concerned with the hermeneutical debate currently centred upon Genesis 1–11. Because these chapters have played such a formative role in theological discussion, it is not surprising that they should have assumed so much importance to interpreters who are concerned to relate the biblical text to modern issues. The interesting thing is that these interpreters represent mainstream international Old Testament scholarship, and are thus an indication of a new direction in which biblical studies are moving.

Chapter 3 is a treatment of the text of Genesis 1–11 from the more familiar perspective of the historical-critical method, with particular attention to translation, source-critical and inter-literary questions. The aim of both chapters is to enable readers to engage closely with the biblical text, both at the level of larger, hermeneutical questions and at that of smaller, detailed points.

I wish to record my thanks to my colleague David Clines for the loan of several books and for helpful suggestions and comments, and to Rosalind and Mandy for typing the manuscript.

ABBREVIATIONS

ANET	*Ancient Near Eastern Texts Relating to the Old Testament* (ed. J.B. Pritchard)
BZAW	Beihefte zur *Zeitschrift für die alttestamentliche Wissenschaft*
FRLANT	Forschungen zur Religion und Literatur des Alten und Neuen Testaments
GNB	Good News Bible
HTR	*Harvard Theological Review*
JBL	*Journal of Biblical Literature*
JSOT	*Journal for the Study of the Old Testament*
JSOTS	Journal for the Study of the Old Testament Supplement Series
JTS	*Journal of Theological Studies*
NEB	New English Bible
REB	Revised English Bible
RSV	Revised Standard Version
VT	*Vetus Testamentum*
WMANT	Wissenschaftliche Monographien zum Alten und Neuen Testament
ZAW	*Zeitschrift für die alttestamentliche Wissenschaft*
ZTK	*Zeitschrift für Theologie und Kirche*

1

GENESIS 1–11
IN CONTEXT

A HUNDRED YEARS AGO, the main concern of biblical scholarship was to reconcile Genesis 1–11 with the scientific discoveries of the nineteenth century. In the 1970s and 1980s its main concern has been to interpret Genesis 1–11 in the light of liberation theology, feminist theology and the ecological crisis.

This statement may surprise readers for several reasons. First, many church-goers, while not taking Genesis literally, believe that the Bible gives us information about the origin and purpose of the universe. Does modern scholarship have nothing to say about this? Many schools and college courses, not to mention their textbooks, interpret Genesis 1–11 in the light of the ancient Near Eastern background. They study the meaning of 'myth' and they compare Genesis 1–11 with parallel texts from ancient Mesopotamia. What has happened to this approach in recent academic study? Some readers will find it hard to believe that academic biblical scholars are being influenced by such things as liberation theology or the ecological crisis. They may go further and say that for scholars to have such interests is to betray the integrity of academic study.

The purpose of this first chapter is to sketch the movement of interpretation from its concern with science 100 years ago, through its attention to the ancient Near Eastern background, to the present engagement with contemporary issues. This will introduce the very complex situation that exists at present in the interpretation of Genesis 1–11, and it will also show that, basically, scholars today are doing what all scholars have done

in the past hundred years: they are interpreting the text from
their own situation or context.

Genesis 1–11 and science
The exploration of the world by sailors in the fifteenth to eigh-
teenth centuries indicated that Genesis 10 could no longer be
regarded as an authoritative account of the geographical dis-
position of the world and its peoples. However, at the beginning
of the nineteenth century it was still generally believed that
Genesis 1 could be shown to be in perfect harmony with scientific discoveries, and that Genesis 2–3 was a true story about
the earliest ancestors of the human race. Calvin's view, that
Genesis 1 was an account of the creation from the standpoint
of a Hebrew observer and not a modern scientific account
(Calvin 1965, pp. 79, 86), was overlooked.

Scientific discoveries in the form of the geology of the 1820s
and 1830s and Darwin's theory of natural selection (1859 and
1870) challenged the early chapters of Genesis on two points.
First, the world was seen to be many thousands (*sic*) of years
old, as against one influential reconstruction of the biblical
chronology which yielded a figure of 4004 BCE for the creation
of the world. However, this was not too damaging. It was possible to understand the six days of creation as six eras, as had
been done by interpreters for many centuries. The implications of Darwin's theories were more disturbing, for they
directly contradicted the biblical account. Whereas the latter
told the story of the creation of the first human beings by God,
and of their fall from a state of paradise to the hard conditions
of the ancient world, the theory of evolution required that the
human race had developed from lower forms of life, and that
its history was one of uninterrupted progress. As the nineteenth century came to an end, the attempt of critical, theological scholarship to interpret Genesis in the light of scientific
discovery was exemplified by S.R. Driver (cf. Rogerson 1984,
pp. 282-23). He put forward the proposal that the Bible has an
outer and an inner sense. Its outer sense was its narrative
form, expressed in terms of the ideas and language of the
ancient world. Its inner sense was a revealed truth which
criticism of the outer sense could in no way affect. Driver rec-
onciled Genesis 3 to the theory of evolution by assuming that

the human race or its separate branches had been faced with a moral choice that would affect its future, and that the wrong choice was made (Driver 1904, pp. 56-57).

Genesis 1–11 and the ancient Near East
Driver was interpreting Genesis 1–11 from his standpoint as a churchman and a critical scholar; we may call this standpoint his context. Even as he worked, the context for the study of Genesis 1–11 was changing. The change resulted from the discovery and decipherment of original texts from ancient Mesopotamia beginning from the late 1840s.

Biblical scholars had long known from writers of Greek antiquity that the Babylonians possessed creation stories similar in some respects to that in Genesis 1. They regarded these stories as dependent on that found in Genesis. But from 1876 newly discovered Babylonian accounts of creation began to be published (see Delano 1985, pp. 52ff.), and the view began to emerge that Genesis 1 was dependent on the Babylonian accounts and not *vice versa*. Further, in 1872 the discovery of a Babylonian version of the flood had been announced.

A new context for the interpretation of Genesis 1–11 began to emerge, a context in which these chapters were no longer seen as the beginning of a sacred, inspired book, the Bible. Instead, they were seen as ancient Hebrew narratives similar to other narratives from the ancient world about cosmic and human origins. If the task of Driver had been to interpret Genesis 1–11 for Christian faith, the task of interpretation in the new context was to discover how ancient Israel had used traditions from the ancient world to express its distinctive faith. Thus in the new context the concern was with the *beliefs* of Israel's official religion. It remained for theologians to make of this what they could for contemporary Christian belief.

Within the context of the view that the stories of Genesis 1–11 were Israelite versions of ancient traditions, several positions emerged. Three of these may be mentioned. At one extreme, it was argued that the alleged dependence of Genesis on Babylonian traditions robbed Genesis of any claim to authority for Christian believers (Delitzsch, 1903). At the other extreme, some scholars in Britain and Scandinavia found in Genesis 1 a link with the New Testament teaching about

death and resurrection, arguing that it was a liturgy used at
the New Year festival when the Israelite kings suffered ritual
death and resurrection. This pattern of death and resurrection
was also held to be present in the Psalms and in Isa. 52.13–
53.12, making possible a link between the suffering, royal
Messiah of the Old Testament and the crucified and risen
Messiah of the New Testament (Bentzen, 1970). A different
viewpoint was that exemplified by the German scholar von
Rad (in Anderson 1984, pp. 53-64). Von Rad held that Israel
took over the idea of creation from its neighbours in the
ancient world quite late in its religious development, and that
the salvation of Israel in the exodus event was more fundamental to Israelite belief than faith in creation. The effect of
this position was to shift attention away from Genesis 1–11
and to emphasize the traditions about God's election and salvation of Israel. Israel knew its God first as redeemer and only
later came to confess that he was Lord of the universe.

A new context
A feature of Old Testament studies in the last twenty years has
been a growth in the number of methods applied to its interpretation. Many of these methods have come from other disciplines. Old Testament scholars have, for example, taken over
from modern literary theory, sociology and social anthropology such approaches as structuralism, close reading and a
renewed interest in the social background to the Bible.

Some of these methods have been applied to Genesis 1–11. At
the same time, there has been a new regard for the authority
of Genesis 1–11, even if this has sometimes been in a back-
handed sort of way. For example, some feminist theologians
have argued that the interpretation of Genesis 3 in terms of
female subordination to males is a distortion of the true
meaning of the text. As will be outlined later, they have argued
for an interpretation that stresses the equality or complement-
arity of the sexes; and in so doing they have implicitly asserted
the authority of Genesis 3 for Christian practice. On the other
hand, more radical feminists have used the biblical text in
order to penetrate behind it to discover a suppressed women's
history with which they can identify themselves. This rejection of the surface meaning of the text has been a back-handed

acknowledgment of its authority, at least for a male-oriented Church and society. Similarly, liberation theology has either re-asserted the authority of the text looked at from a liberation perspective, or has rejected its surface meaning in a search for the history of the oppressed.

The present context in which Genesis 1–11 is being interpreted is thus characterized by two features: a growth in the number of methods applied to the study of these chapters, and a renewed interest in the relevance of Genesis 1–11 for such questions as the rights of the oppressed and poor, the status of women and the ecological crisis. In the case of the last of these, Old Testament study has been responding to those ecologists who have argued that the command to humanity in Gen. 1.26ff. to subdue the earth is the cause of the crisis that we face. In becoming sensitive to some or all of these issues, academic biblical studies have been moving into a new context, a context that has affected the interpretation of Genesis 1–11 as profoundly as the discovery of Babylonian texts affected interpretation at the end of the nineteenth century.

One difference between the present context and previous contexts is the greater diversity of methods and approaches that characterizes the present situation. To conclude this chapter, an attempt will be made to summarize these. This summary will then form the basis for a more detailed exposition in the next chapter. Full references are given in the next chapter to the works briefly mentioned here.

1. Literary-critical readings with contemporary implications

The work of Catholic scholars such as Lohfink, Beauchamp and Zenger has concentrated upon those parts of Genesis 1–11 traditionally assigned to the Priestly source of the Pentateuch. The conclusions of these scholars have, however, been of greatest interest in the light of the current concern with ecological matters. Lohfink, taking up a suggestion first made by McEvenue, has argued that P is written from a 'pacifist' standpoint, and that this must affect the interpretation of passages such as Gen. 1.26ff. regarding the human domination of the world. Lohfink argues that Gen. 1.26ff. gives no sanction to domination and exploitation. Beauchamp's discussion deals

with human relations with the animal creation, while Zenger,
in his discussion of the 'bow' in Gen. 9.13 explicitly addresses
ecological questions in a work which is a detailed example of
traditional literary criticism.

2. Literary readings

Literary readings are of various kinds. They may be concerned with the whole of Genesis 1–11 or only with parts of it;
and they may be either thematic or structuralist. Clines
applies the concept of 'theme' to Genesis 1–11, arguing that
the content of the chapters can be described in two ways: a.
humankind's tendency to destroy what God has made good, b.
God's ability to overcome humanity's destructive tendencies.
He opts for the latter theme in the light of the Pentateuch as a
whole. Structuralist readings of Genesis 2–3 occupied a whole
issue of *Semeia* in 1980 (Patte, 1980). The various contributors
were agreed in regarding the text as mysterious and multi-
layered, and their aim was to make some of this depth apparent. Jobling used the opposing categories of inside/outside to
illumine the text.
    Literary readings differ from other approaches in being a-
historical. Whereas Lohfink, for example, locates the P source
in a specific historical setting, literary interpreters are concerned with the inner dynamics of the text itself, and not necessarily with reference to reality outside the text.

3. Liberation readings

At least three approaches can be distinguished here. The first,
exemplified by scholars such as Louise Schottroff and Wittenberg, is essentially historical-critical, but with a different
emphasis from that of Lohfink and his colleagues. The latter
deal much more closely with the details of the text. Schottroff
and Wittenberg gain their impetus more from what they pre-
sume the social background to have been than from the text
itself. Thus Wittenberg regards the Yahwist source (J) as anti-
Solomonic propaganda and sees in Genesis 3 and in Genesis 11
a condemnation of Solomon's wisdom and of his building
activities. Mosala also sets out from historical-critical recon-

structions of the setting of texts, but is more interested in what the text conceals than in what it says. Historical criticism is used by Mosala to recover a lost history of the oppressed. Boesak's liberation reading of Genesis 4 is an existential reading that takes the narrative about Cain and Abel as a story with universal application.

4. Feminist readings

Two different approaches can be noted here. Trible, in her classic *God and the Rhetoric of Sexuality*, uses an essentially literary approach; yet this has a specific purpose, which is not simply to explore the dimensions of Genesis 2–3 for their own sake, but to argue a feminist case. Myers uses the latest research on the sociology of women in Israelite highland agriculture as the key to understanding Genesis 2–3.

5. Genesis 1–11 and ancient Near Eastern texts

This section comes last deliberately. It would be wrong to suggest that scholars no longer interpret Genesis 1–11 against the ancient Near Eastern background. On the other hand, this has become only one of many possible approaches, and it is sometimes used by writers who fall into the categories earlier mentioned in this chapter. While it is valuable in providing a contrast between the faith of Israel and that of Israel's neighbours, it does not provide an obvious link with contemporary problems.

The approaches just outlined will now receive detailed attention.

2

APPROACHES
TO GENESIS 1–11

1. Literary-critical readings with contemporary implications

IN A SERIES OF detailed studies of the Priestly source of the Pentateuch or, more exactly, what he calls P^g (the Priestly historical narrative: the 'g' stands for the German *Geschichts-erzählung*, which means historical narrative), N. Lohfink has suggested some striking interpretations of parts of Genesis 1–11. He believes that P^g was composed toward the end of the exile, and was intended to present an account of Israel's history deliberately different from the Yahwist's history and the Deuteronomic history (Lohfink 1983, pp. 55-56). The writer of P^g wished Israel to be a temple-based community centred upon the presence of God and governed by sacred rituals and sacrifices in such a way that no one would exercise power over others. The frictions and stresses within the society that would normally lead to bloodshed were to be removed by the use of sacrifice to restore the broken relationships. P^g rejected the notion of war, a fact indicated, according to Lohfink, by its treatment of the exodus and of the mode of possession by the Israelites of the land of Canaan. Whereas J and D indicate a military defeat of Egypt and a warlike occupation of Canaan, P^g has no account of Egypt's military demise at the exodus, describes Israel as a sacral and not a military body in the wilderness, and represents the occupation of Canaan as the peaceful setting up of God's sanctuary in the land. (See Lohfink 1982, pp. 194-99 for an account in English of some of these points.)

Seen in the light of the whole of P^g, those parts of this source that are found in Genesis 1–11 have a clear message. It is noteworthy, first, that in Gen. 1.26-30 humankind is not given permission to eat meat. This permission comes only after the flood, at Gen. 9.3-4. According to Lohfink the ideal implied in Gen. 1.26-30 is that humans will not exercise force over the animal creation. However, in the view of P^g, humankind did not hold to this ideal, and this was why God brought the flood upon the earth. The situation after the flood is a compromise. Humans are given permission to eat meat; but this is not a mandate for the exploitation of animals. The reason for the permission to eat meat is that Israel can offer to God the sacrifices that will enable order to be maintained in a sacral, oppression-free community.

Lohfink also argues strongly that the Hebrew verb *rādâ* in Gen. 1.28, usually rendered 'to have dominion over', has the basic sense of 'to wander around'. Its semantic field includes 'accompany', 'pasture', 'guide', 'lead', 'rule' and 'command', from which it is clear that its meaning of 'to rule' has to be understood in the context of shepherding. Thus the task given to humanity in Gen. 1.28 in relation to the rest of the created order is to be a shepherd (Lohfink 1977, pp. 167-68; English in Lohfink 1982, pp. 178-79). With regard to the command to be fruitful and multiply, Lohfink argues that in the light of P^g as a whole this must be taken as a command limited to the establishment of the families of the earth and of their possession of their own lands. The command has nothing to do with the modern notion of continuous growth:

> There was once growth; not, there must always be growth. The goal of growth was simply that the nations would come from the original families. They now exist; and as a result the blessing of growth has achieved its goal (Lohfink 1977, p. 185 my translation; see also Lohfink 1982, p. 196 for an English version).

Lohfink's treatment of parts of Genesis 1–11 anchors these texts firmly in the situation of post-exilic Israel. Genesis 1 becomes a prophetic text, depicting an ideal which no longer exists: an ideal of human society in which there is no war, and no exploitation of the created order, and in which human responsibility is to act as a shepherd to the created order.

However, the picture presented by P^g, although a compromise with the violent realities of human nature, is nonetheless an attempt to create an oppression-free society based upon sacral institutions. Although Lohfink does not draw conclusions from this about how we should order the world today, his exegesis rules out interpretations which are commonly heard today: e.g. that Genesis 1–11 teaches us that we live in a world created by God which he has described as 'good'; or that Genesis 1 is responsible for the human exploitation of the natural world. (This last charge could be true, of course, if misinterpretations of Gen. 1.28 had been responsible.)

It is likely that Lohfink's suggestions will strike a chord with many modern readers; and the implications of this will be discussed elsewhere in this book. For the moment, it is sufficient to observe that the questions to which Lohfink is sensitive are questions relevant to the end of the twentieth century, and indicate how the contemporary situation can interact with work of a rigorous literary-critical nature.

Beauchamp (1987, pp. 139-82), in a complex and subtle essay, follows Lohfink in some respects; but his essay concentrates upon the tension between Gen. 1.26-30 and Gen. 9.1-7; and to that extent it avoids the criticism that he is interpreting not the text of Genesis 1–11 but sources that have been hypothetically isolated by scholars. The differences between Gen. 1.26-30 and Gen. 9.1-7 are that, in the former, humans are not permitted to eat animals, whereas in the latter, not only is this permission given, but language is used about the relation between humans and animals that implies a significant increase in human domination. Gen. 9.2 says that the fear of humankind shall be upon every beast of the earth, etc., and that they will be *delivered* into the hand (or power) of human beings. This last phrase is one which is used elsewhere in the Old Testament to describe God's giving victory over his enemies. But not only does Gen. 9.1-7 envisage the human consumption of animals; it envisages the killing of human beings by human beings, and it seeks to restrict such killing by allowing the execution of murderers, on the grounds that humankind is made in God's image.

Beauchamp argues that in these two texts (and elsewhere in the Old Testament) the animals act as a sign indicating the nature of humanity, and humankind's relationship to the created order. The regime of Gen. 1.26-30 does not propose vegetarianism for its own sake. The vegetarianism helps to define what it means to say that humanity is made in God's image; for this language is about relationships with the animals, as is evident from Gen. 1.26, 'Let us make...in our image...and let them have dominion...' This dominion is characterized by tenderness towards the animals, and since no animal blood is to be shed by human beings, it is also implied that humans do not shed each other's blood and that animals do not shed that of other animals (cf. 1.30). What is implied in Gen. 1.26-30 is elaborated in Gen. 9.1-7, in the changed circumstances of the post-flood world. In place of tenderness towards animals on the part of humanity there is now warlike domination. If the animals experienced tenderness in Gen. 1.26-30 they now experience fear and dread (9.2). It is implied that animals will seek to kill human beings (v. 5b) and so each other, and that human beings will be like animals in that regard. The only difference will be that the extent of human beings' killing each other will be limited by the right of execution of murderers. This is because humankind is created in God's image.

From the contrast between Gen. 1.26-30 and 9.1-7 it is clear, in Beauchamp's view, that mankind is no longer in the image of God as defined in Genesis 1. Humanity's relationship to animals has changed from that of tenderness to that of domination; from that of the shepherd to the hunter. Humans have become more like the animals, not only through murders and war, but through the enslavement of human by human. Thus Gen. 1.26-30 is a text expressing an ideal:

> It is able to believe that a mastery over the earth is possible without exercising a mastery over the other beings, who are intermediate beings between the master and the earth. Genesis 1 teaches us that there is only true mastery over the earth if mankind does not enslave itself by enslaving its fellows (p. 170).

As such, it has much in common with prophetic texts that see a new creation as including peace between the animals and between the animals and humanity (see Isa. 65.17-25).

> The Bible does not think of peace between human beings without
> peace between human and animal (p. 180).

Beauchamp's stress on human relations with animals as an
important sign enables him to make other illuminating comparisons. For example, in Lev. 26.21-22 one of the penalties for
disobedience on the part of Israel is that God will bring wild
animals to devour their crops and their children. Thus, animals will be a sign of disobedience and judgment. In Genesis
10, those parts belonging to P^g and containing the words, 'by
their families, languages, their lands and their nations' (vv. 5,
20, 31), suggest a differentiation of the human race into an
equivalent of the species (kinds) that characterize the animals;
if so, the greater stress on the (violent) animal constituent of
humankind after the flood is indicated.

Like that of Lohfink, Beauchamp's exposition is firmly
anchored in what he believes parts of Genesis 1–11 meant to
the Priestly circles who were revising the outlook of Israel's
earlier traditions; and again, it is one which is bound to be read
with sympathy in our contemporary world. For while there is
no reason why we should give precedence to the viewpoint of
P^g over against that of other strands of the Old Testament, we
are strongly tempted to do so by our modern concerns, and we
are once again entitled to conclude that these concerns have
not been without influence upon Beauchamp's work.

An interesting feature of Zenger's detailed and subtle monograph (Zenger, 1983) is the fact that he mentions the current
ecological crisis several times at the beginning of his work, and
devotes a brief concluding section to 'some ecological-theologi-
cal implications' (pp. 179-83). Here is another work of traditional literary-critical study which is explicitly sensitive to an
important modern issue.

There are many similarities between Zenger's approach
and those of Lohfink and Beauchamp. Like Lohfink, Zenger
assigns parts of Genesis 1–11 to the Priestly narrative (P^g)
and interprets these in the light of his view of the narrative as
a whole. Like Beauchamp, he sees the relation between Gen.
1.26-30 and 9.1-3, 7 as a crucial issue in interpretation. However, he disagrees with Lohfink about the extent of P^g and,
against Beauchamp, regards 9.4-6 as a later addition to P^g.

Zenger accepts the view proposed by Wellhausen, and supported by 'the majority of recent publications' (p. 41) that P^g ends at Deut. 34.7-9, that is, with the death of Moses. This enables him to argue that three figures are crucial in P^g— Adam, Abraham and Moses—and that P^g is to be divided into two main parts, Gen. 1.1 to Exod. 1.7 and Exod. 1.13 to Deut. 34.9. Although he has a different view from Lohfink and others about the importance of the occupation of the land of Canaan in P^g (Lohfink sees Josh. 19.41 as the ending of P^g), Zenger's conclusions have much in common with those of Lohfink:

> P^g is the programmatic outline for a non-political Israel, which regards the gift of a communal experience of God's nearness as the most important of all benefits, rather than being a state and having its own land. As such, P^g does not attempt to present a detailed and realizable constitution, such as is found in Ezekiel 40–48. It is a basic reflection on the presupposition and purpose of a new manifestation of Israel, that is to become the medium of the mighty activity of the creator God who gives life (pp. 45-46).

Written towards the end of the sixth century, probably in Babylon (although Jerusalem remains a possibility), P^g offers to the community the chance to realize, in its religious life, its status as a community fulfilling the purpose of the creation. This was once upon a time achieved in the period from Abraham to Sinai, and the status of the community, as being in life-giving relationship to Yahweh, was embodied in the Sinai covenant. Thereafter, the history of Israel was a history of failure to become, in the promised land, what it had been. However, this history of sin and failure did not threaten the creation, because God had already made the created order so secure that it could not be threatened.

This view of the purpose of P^g brings us to one of the central claims that Zenger makes about those parts of Genesis 1–11 that belong to P^g. Discussing the relation between the creation and flood stories and between Gen. 1.26-30 and 9.1-3, 7, he argues that both, taken together, constitute the account of creation as it impinged upon the world of P^g. He does not deny that there are differences between these passages. Gen. 1.26 describes a shepherd-like function for humankind which is strengthened after the flood. Also, the flood to some extent

damages the earth as long as the waters remain. There is a
new 'realism' after the flood, one which recognizes that the
world contains violence and injustice.

Yet, when all this has been allowed, Zenger's emphasis is
more upon continuity than discontinuity. Even if the world
implied in Gen. 1.26-30 alone no longer exists, if it ever did, the
world implied in Genesis 1 and Gen. 9.1-3, 7 taken together
does exist, and offers to Israel the hope of life lived in close
relationship with the creator God. After the flood, there is not a
new creation of the world, but rather, the beginning of a new
era for a purified world. It is at this point that we must consider Zenger's treatment of Gen. 9.1-3, 7 and of the bow in the
clouds which God promises to set (9.13). He begins by noting
that the language of 9.2—'the fear of you and the dread of you
shall be upon every beast of the earth'—is not the language of
war, but that of God's gift of the land of Canaan to his people
(Exod. 23.27ff., 'I will send my terror before you...I will drive
them out from before you'). Gen. 9.1-3 therefore adds to the
idea of Gen. 1.26ff. the idea that humankind must shepherd
the animals: that is, it imposes the additional charge to be the
lord of the created order, in other words, so to rule over it that
the weaker and threatened animals will be protected. Gen. 9.1-
3, then, does not abolish Gen. 1.26ff. but strengthens it.

The bow in the clouds is not a sign of peace and reconciliation
but a sign that over and above humanity stands the protector
of the created order: the creator God who will protect his creation from all that would destroy it. Zenger points out that, in
the Old Testament, it is a broken bow that is the sign of peace
(Ps. 46.9; Zech. 9.10). This does not compromise the 'pacifist'
nature of P[g]. The bow is not a summons to war or a justification of it. Rather, it is a call to trust in the determination and
ability of God to safeguard his creation.

In the concluding section on ecological implications, Zenger
makes the following points. For P[g] the history of Israel is
inseparable from the story of creation, as is also the history of
the Church. What God does in order to redeem his people is
part of what he is doing to preserve the life of his creation.
Thus humanity is an integral part of creation in the sense that
humankind 'either survives with the created order by living in
harmony with it, or goes under with the created order by liv-

ing against it' (p. 179). Second, humanity is given responsibility for the created order and is answerable to the creator God. This answerability, according to P^g, is to be established by Israel's building of a sanctuary where the creator God will reveal himself to humankind. The people of God is called to live an exemplary life in this regard, so that the earth will be a place of life for all that lives.

To the extent that humans destroy the earth as a place of life, they lose their humanity:

> A human race that regards the earth as material for satisfying its own needs, that uses animals as creatures without rights, that makes power the criterion for decisions (and only reflects later on the morality of what has been done), that produces weapons that can destroy the ecological balance of the world completely—such a human race is acting contrary to creation and is on the way to becoming the 'all flesh' (which had 'corrupted its way') of which Genesis 6.12 speaks (p. 180).

The bow in the sky, then, is a sign of hope to a suffering world, witnessing to the royal sovereignty over the earth of the creator God.

Zenger's final point stems from his views about the tent sanctuary whose construction P^g describes (Exod. 25ff.) as a place where God meets his people in their worship on the seventh day. The stone-built temples of Solomon and the ancient world were symbols of political might and of the oppression of the poorer classes. The cult to be celebrated in the tent (Lev. 9) is neither the state cult of Solomon, which legitimized power, nor the priestly dominated orgiastic cult of Canaan and Egypt. In both cases, the priestly cult degraded the participation of the people. What is envisaged by P^g is a cult for the whole community, whose sacrificial offerings are a thankful rendering to the creator God of what he has given to his people. For the modern world, this indicates responsibility for creation flowing from a common life rooted in worship and centred on the meaning of creation, which consideration becomes the criterion for the ordering of daily life. We shall return to Zenger's rich monograph in other sections of the book. This summary has been restricted to the treatment of Genesis 1–11 and to the ecological implications.

2. Literary readings

Literary readings of Genesis 1–11 differ from the literary-
critical readings that we have been considering in at least two
ways. First, they ignore the sources that are presupposed by
literary-critical approaches; second, they hold that the important thing about the narratives is not their presumed setting in
a particular period of Israelite history, but their internal
dynamics of plot, characterization and theme.

Although doubt continues to be expressed about the possibility or propriety of dividing Genesis 1–11 into sources, the
attempt to do so is not without good grounds. Leaving aside the
striking differences between the use of the divine name in Gen.
1.1–2.4a and 2.4b–3.24 we may note two apparent contradictions. If Gen. 1.26-30 does not allow human beings to kill animals, why does Abel offer sheep as a sacrifice to God, and why
does God accept the sacrifice (4.4)? If the human race was not
divided into nations and scattered abroad speaking different
languages until after the building of the tower of Babel (11.1-
9), why do 10.5, 20 and 31 speak of the languages and lands of
the various peoples listed? Two possible answers can be given
by those reading the final form of the text in a literary way.
First, Gen. 1.26-30 may have to be read in the light of 4.4, with
the conclusion that the former text does not, at the very least,
exclude killing animals in order to sacrifice them. Second, the
apparently contradictory arrangement of Genesis 10–11 may
be of significance for the interpretation of the whole (see
below). The strength of the second answer, which gives pref-
erence to the text as a whole as opposed to trying to divide it
into sources in order to remove contradictions, is that source
division is always bound to be hypothetical, whereas the final
form of the text is a reality.

Of the various possible literary readings this section will deal
with those of Clines (1978) and Jobling (1980). In the course of
his study of the 'theme' of the Pentateuch, Clines considers the
question of what might be said to be the 'theme' of Genesis 1–
11. Drawing upon the work of standard commentators such
as von Rad and Westermann, Clines considers several possible
themes. The first is a sin–speech–mitigation–punishment
theme. He shows that in each of five episodes, those of the fall

(ch. 3), Cain and Abel (ch. 4), the sons of God (6.1-4), the flood (6.5–7.24), and the tower of Babel (11.1-9), before God punishes the evildoers there is a divine speech and a mitigation of the punishment *before* the punishment is administered. Thus, in 3.21 God clothes the humans with skins following his speech in 3.14-19 and prior to driving Adam and Eve from the garden in 3.22-24. In ch. 4, God puts a protecting mark upon Cain (v. 15) following his speech in vv. 10-11 and Cain's departure to the land of Nod in v. 16. In the flood story we are told that Noah found favour in God's eyes (6.8) following God's speech announcing judgment in 6.6-7.

The tower of Babel is an interesting case, because Clines implies that the mitigation is in 10.1-32, i.e. that it precedes the tower of Babel story (p. 63); and later (p. 68) he argues that, if 10.1-32 were placed after 11.1-9, the passage would have to be read under the sign of judgment rather than as a fulfilment of the renewed command of 9.1 to be fruitful and multiply. This illustrates how a literary approach deals with the problem on which source critics base their detection of sources.

Clines rejects the sin–speech–mitigation–punishment scheme as the overall 'theme' of Genesis 1–11, because it cannot include the creation or the genealogies. Rather Clines accepts that it is a recurrent *motif*. He next tries a spread of sin, spread of grace theme. This draws attention to the way in which wrongdoing escalates from the sin of Adam and Eve through the violence of Cain and Lamech to the generation destroyed by the flood; and after the flood there is an escalation from Noah's family to the building of the tower of Babel. In each case, God responds graciously. God does not kill Adam and Eve, he puts he a protecting mark upon Cain and he commands Noah to build an ark. The sequel to the tower of Babel is the growth of the nations (10.1-32), which account comes before the tower of Babel story so as to be seen as a sign of grace. Clines also incorporates the creation narrative and the genealogies by arguing that the former expresses a series of gracious acts which balance the pessimism of some of the subsequent narratives; and that the genealogies, by emphasizing the continual presence of death, imply also God's grace which enables life to continue.

Clines then explores a further possible theme, that of creation–uncreation–recreation. He notes that, in the flood story, some of the boundaries fixed in Genesis 1 are removed in order to allow the waters to cover the earth. The flood is finally restrained by the re-imposition of the boundaries. This approach then yields the suggestion that the flood story is only the culmination of a process of undoing of the creation which is discernible in chs. 3–6. After the flood, the process of uncreation begins again, as the narrative moves through the strife within Noah's family to the dispersion of the human race after the building of the tower of Babel. The combination of the sin and grace theme with the creation, uncreation theme enables Clines to propose as the most comprehensive theme that of the unfailing grace of God in the face of human sin, even when that sin brings the creation to the brink of uncreation.

Clines's literary reading yields many insights. It is also noteworthy that it is explicitly theological and not related to modern problems as are the modern readings outlined in the previous section. Indeed, Clines goes out of his way to emphasize that a literary reading offers the text as story:

> What is offered in the story is a 'world'—make-believe or real, familiar or unfamiliar. To the degree that the hearer or reader of the story is imaginatively seized by the story, to that degree he or she 'enters' the world of the story. That means that the reader of the story, when powerfully affected by it, becomes a participant of its world. One learns, by familiarity with the story, one's way about its world until it becomes one's own world too (p. 102).

And again:

> The Pentateuch becomes...a source of life, not by being fed through some hermeneutical machine that prints out contemporary answers to contemporary questions, but through the reader's patient engagement with the text and openness to being seized, challenged, or threatened by the 'world' it lays bare (p. 118).

Clines discusses motifs that are apparent on the surface of the text of Genesis 1–11, and seeks to find an organizing principle that would encompass their interrelation and their potential for development. Structuralist readings are more concerned with levels of meaning below the surface; however, when these levels are described, they inevitably affect our appreciation of what is going on at the surface level.

In the 1980 *Semeia* symposium on Genesis 2–3, Jobling proposes the opposition of inside/outside as a clue to the semantics of the passage. The story begins with God's introducing the man (from outside) into the garden, and ends with the human beings outside the garden. The story takes place inside the garden, but to be inside the garden is to be in an almost dangerous situation. It contains a serpent who is a source of temptation as well as trees whose prohibition is a potential source of danger. Life inside the garden differs greatly from that outside. Inside the garden, agriculture is easy, but it is the only occupation. If the garden contains animals, these are not bred or used by the man. Although he has a female companion there is no other society; neither is there sexual awareness or sexual reproduction. Although inside there is immortality, it is an immortality of a non-societal monochrome variety.

All this is in contrast with the outside, the world familiar to human beings, with difficult agriculture, but with husbandry and hunting in addition to agriculture and a larger society based upon sexual awareness and procreation.

According to this reading the story functions to enable men to cope with women and with the harshness of agricultural life. Men may face hard work and death and may yearn for immortality and ease. But these latter ideals, when available to the first man in the garden of Eden, were not without danger and disadvantage. Woman plays a complex role in the story. Created out of the man's rib to provide the companionship no animal could provide, she nonetheless pursues independent action, until she becomes largely responsible for man's being outside the garden. She is thus part of man, but enables man to argue that expulsion from the garden was not his fault. The story enables man both to long for the lost life of the garden, and to prefer the realities of his present existence.

Although this type of analysis is based wholly upon the text, it does refer to realities outside the text, namely, human awareness of the contradiction between dream and reality. It assumes a setting in a non-specified Israelite or even universal human situation, it does not provide theological truths and it is male-orientated as are some of the other structuralist readings, although this does not mean that such approaches are necessarily sexist. Yet it enables readers to see the text in new ways, and indicates how difficult it is to exhaust a text of its possibilities of meaning.

3. Liberation readings

Liberation readings of the Bible take a number of forms. Some are literary-critical readings which describe situations in the life of ancient Israel, but which attempt an application to modern situations. Others simply use the historical situation in Israel to establish common ground between the Old Testament situations and modern conditions, and assume that the biblical text can then address the modern conditions directly. Another approach assumes the unitariness of human nature, so that the biblical narrative has universal application. Finally, there is the approach that goes behind the text to discover a suppressed history of oppressed people.

Wittenberg (1988) dates the J parts of Genesis 2–11 to the Solomonic era, and sees the J work as part of a theological critique of Solomon's reign. He notes that various scholars have detected royal motifs in Genesis 2–3, and he suggests that the garden of Eden was reminiscent of the Solomonic royal park, that the serpent could be connected with a serpent cult in Jerusalem which was later abolished by Hezekiah (2 Kgs 18.4), and that the cherubim guarding the garden of Eden could be an allusion to the cherubim in the temple which protected the ark. We could add that the tradition in Ezek. 28.11-19 which in many respects is so similar to Genesis 3 is also concerned with a royal figure.

Given these royal allusions, Wittenberg reads Genesis 2–3 as an attack upon the reign of Solomon. Adam is a royal figure whose undoing results from his desire to know good and evil apart from God. The reign of Solomon resulted in a royal reorganization of the whole society, which brought great hardship upon the people and the break-down of society as it had been previously organized. Just as in Genesis 2–11 the 'fall' of Adam had brought about an increase in violence, with Cain killing Abel and Lamech exacting vengeance far in excess of his grievance, so the desire of Solomon to determine what was right led to violence and to the loss of social cohesion.

Wittenberg argues further that the genealogies in Genesis 10 emphasize socio-economic differences between prosperous cities such as Erech (Uruk), Accad (Agade), and Nineveh, cities that belonged to the list of Ham, and the tribal societies that belonged to the list of Shem. Thus the lists contrast the centralized city states with the de-centralized tribal peoples. The standpoint of the J writer is that of the tribal peoples, whereas Solomon, contrary to the traditions of his people, created a centralized state. The story of the tower of Babel is an attack upon the building activity of Solomon, with the king wanting to create a reputation by his great building works. The only result of this was to place such a strain upon his kingdom that it divided after his death in the same way that the building of the tower of Babel resulted in the division of the people.

Wittenberg isolates a strand in Genesis 1–11 which is critical of the centralization and the misuse of power. He assigns special importance to this strand for Christian usage by claiming that, 'in the crucified Jesus the resistance theology of the Solomonic age received its ultimate vindication' (p. 17). Louise Schottroff (1988, pp. 8-26) gives a social-historical reading of Gen. 1.1–2.4a, placing the account in the presumed situation of the deported Jewish farmers and craftsmen living in exile in Babylon after the fall of Jerusalem in 587 BCE. She assumes the correctness of the account of the circumstances of the Jews as worked out by W. Schottroff (1983, pp. 122-28), according to which the deported craftsmen had no chance to pass on their skills to their families, and where some Jews were enslaved to rich families. Believing that the social setting of the text is a clue to its meaning, she notes that Genesis 1 describes God as a craftsman fashioning the world. She also notes that God is depicted both as a mother bird and as a sovereign king. Schottroff next contrasts the beauty of the original creation with the polluted and threatened world we live in today. She contrasts our experience of the creation story with that of its original readers. For them, in their oppression and hopelessness, the story of creation gave them faith in their

God who had created so much beauty. No one could take from them the contemplation of that beauty.

The verses about humankind's being created in the image of God (Gen. 1.26-27) produce two comments. For the original readers, the exiled Jews, these verses gave hope. In their exile they had no value in the eyes of their overlords other than their economic value. But their sacred traditions assured them that they were made in God's image, and that gave them incomparable value. Schottroff illustrates this with a charming story about Hillel, who, in going to bathe, noted that, since the statues (images) of the Caesars were regularly washed, he also needed to wash. He was greater than a Caesar because he was made in the image of God. For contemporary readers, the question provoked by Gen. 1.26-30 is 'are we going to live as those made in the image of God, or as a race of superhumans?' If the answer is in favour of the former, this will require more than the banishing of environmentally harmful products from our kitchens!

Schottroff's exposition of the relation between man and woman in Gen. 1.26-30 brings us close to a hermeneutics of rejection, that is, a reading which questions the assumptions of the text. She argues that, among the exiles, to have many children was an aspect of liberation by ensuring the continuance of the people and increasing their economic strength. She rejects interpretations of humankind's being made in God's image such as that in 1 Cor. 11.7 according to which only man is the image and glory of God and the woman is related to God only via man. She is also critical of Barth's views that man and woman constitute the divine image in their relationship to each other. This simply sanctions male views of marriage together with their disadvantages to women. Schottroff prefers to interpret language about the image of God as a summons to men and women to work together in equality and justice. But she also feels that the female experience of oppression that this text has caused and sanctioned will enable women to work all the more effectively for the alleviation of every kind of injustice. It is here that we are close to a hermeneutics of rejection, in the sense that the negative effect of the text upon women can be put to positive use. Because the text has been misused in the past to the detriment of women, it needs to be women who assist to understand and use the text appropriately today.

The third example of a liberation reading of part of Genesis 1–11 is Boesak's treatment of Genesis 4, as presented by West (1990, pp. 279-99). Boesak is well known in the West as a leading South African churchman who is engaged in the struggle against apartheid. His reading of Genesis 4 is thus deeply affected by the situation in which he works, and by his belief that the text tells a universal story applicable to all ages:

> The story of Cain and Abel is a story about two types or kinds of people. It is a very human story that is still being enacted today. This story does not tell us in the first place what happened once upon a time; rather, it tells us about something that happens today. Because this story is a human story, we find very human elements in it and elements from our own human history (West, p. 285).

From this standpoint Boesak gives an essentially literary reading of Genesis 4. He notes the repetiton of the word 'brother' in the story of Cain and Abel (vv. 2, 8 [twice], 9 [twice], 10 and 11) as a way of emphasizing the wickedness of Cain's actions. He has killed the human being closest to him and has thereby essentially denied his own humanity, since humanity is a co-operative venture. Cain's punishment is that he is alienated from the land on which he relied for a living (he was a tiller of the ground) and is forced to wander without rest and without a goal.

The continuation of the story in vv. 23-24, where Lamech, Cain's descendant, boasts that he has killed a man for wounding him, shows that as history moves on humans learn nothing, and things do not change. We can add that this might be a justification for the way in which Boesak applies the story universally.

However, the story does not end in complete darkness. Gen. 4.25-26 records the birth of a son to Adam and Eve to replace the murdered Abel, and the chapter ends with the words, 'At that time men began to call upon the name of the Lord'. Boesak comments:

> After murder, after death, after annihilation and inhumanity, God begins again (West, p. 284).

I shall not comment on the way in which Boesak draws parallels between the anxieties experienced by Cain after he has murdered Abel and the anxieties Boesak believes are experienced by those he regards as oppressors in our contemporary world. Whatever one's views on this matter, it is not difficult to see how Boesak's reading can bring hope to people who are being oppressed. The text makes it clear that the oppression of human beings by other human beings is not God's plan for the world, that God pronounces judgment against it, but that he is also at work to bring hope through those who honour his name. Whereas Clines's literary reading is concerned to bring readers into 'the world of the text', there to find the values of their own world challenged, Boesak sees the text as referring to concrete situations in our own world, and is saying to his own people that the oppression they suffer is condemned by God, but that he is even now at work to make things new.

Mosala's reading of the story of Cain and Abel (West, pp. 287ff.) is very different from that of Boesak. He begins from a hermeneutics of suspicion, that is, he does not take the text at its face value but looks behind it to discover its origins within the class struggle in ancient Israel. Such research indicates that Genesis 4 comes from the hand of the ruling class, and that its historical background is the Davidic monarchy, during which there was a relentless dispossession of Israelite village peasants from their lands. Given this setting, the text seeks to justify this dispossession by identifying the peasants with Cain, whose offering God rejected. The idea of the offering to God is a reminder that the village peasants were required to pay crippling tribute to the ruling classes. The death of Abel may well mask a case of successful resistance by a peasant against an attempt of a more wealthy man to appropriate his family lands. That such attempts at appropriation were made is clear from the story of Naboth's vineyard (1 Kgs 21).

Mosala admits that his reading is

> not immediately obvious to the reader. It requires a reading that issues out of a firm grounding in the struggle for liberation, as well as a basis in critical theoretical perspectives which can expose the deep structure of the text (Mosala, cited by West, p. 288).

Basic to his position is his belief that texts which originate from the class of the oppressors cannot be used in the struggle for liberation. If they are, they may undergird the interests of the oppressors even though they are being used by the oppressed. 'Oppressive texts cannot be totally tamed or subverted into liberative texts' (West, p. 293).

Thus read, the biblical text ceases to be an end in itself. It becomes a means to an end, which is to help to reconstruct a history of class struggle with which the oppressed can identify. Further, it makes possible the necessary unmasking both of the oppressive nature of biblical texts and of their interpretation within a Church and an academic community which have represented, and still represent, the interests of élites rather than of oppressed people. While this may sound very strange to those of us who are indeed students of the Bible from within a privileged rather than an oppressed situation, we cannot overlook the intense sincerity of Mosala's position, and reflect that, if we were in the same position, what he is saying might not sound quite so strange.

4. Feminist readings

Feminist readings of the Bible are as diverse as liberation readings. They can range from readings designed to bring out hitherto unnoticed facets of the text, to readings which are similar in their aims and execution to the hermeneutics of suspicion or rejection which we noted above in the work of Mosala and Schottroff (see further Collins, 1985).

A feminist reading of Genesis 2–3 that has become a classic is that of Trible (1978). It is essentially a literary reading with structuralist undertones and it is executed with skill and sensitivity that cannot be adequately conveyed in a brief summary. From a feminist standpoint, its aim is to combat a number of misogynist readings which have 'acquired the status of canonicity', including the view that man is superior to woman for the following reasons: he is created first, the woman is made from the man's rib to be his helper, she is named by the man, is responsible for his downfall, is punished by childbirth because of her greater sin, and in her desire for her husband is to be submissive to him. Trible's strategy is to provide a reading

Genesis 1–11

which rebuts all of these arguments; the following summary
will concentrate upon the alternative reading which she
offers.

Gen. 2.5 states, in the standard translations, that there was
no man to till the ground. On the basis of the pun in v.
7 on the Hebrew words '*ādām* (man) and '*ᵃdāmâ* (earth), Trible renders the Hebrew '*ādām* as 'earth-creature' and maintains
that it is 'neither male or female nor a combination of both'
(p. 98). It is God who, unilaterally, decides that the earth-
creature needs an '*ēzer*, a Hebrew word that here denotes a
companion 'who is neither subordinate or superior; one who
alleviates isolation through identity' (p. 90). Whereas birds
and animals were created from the dust of the earth (2.19),
the '*ēzer* is made from the earth-creature and is thus unique.
When she is brought to the man he does not name her, as he
had named the animals and thus had assumed power over
them. Rather, he recognizes the existence of sexuality.

With the creation of the companion from the material of its
body, the earth-creature becomes a different being: it 'is no
longer identical with its past, so that when next it speaks
[when the companion is brought to it] a different creature is
speaking' (p. 97). This different creature is a male; and it was
not created prior to the female. Both were created simultane-
ously from the earth-creature. 'His sexual identity depends
upon her even as hers depends upon him. For both of them
sexuality originates in the one flesh of humanity' (p. 99).

The scene of the temptation of the woman by the serpent
(Gen. 3.1-7) indicates a continuity between the earth-creature
and the human couple, since the order not to eat from a certain tree was given to the former (2.17). Trible notes that the
serpent uses the second person plural in referring to God's
command (compare 2.17, literally, 'and of the tree of the
knowledge of good and evil *thou* shalt not eat from it' with 3.2,
literally, 'Did God say, "*You* may not eat from any tree of the
garden"?'). This indicates both the unity and the distinction of
the male and female, and although the woman takes the ini-
tiative in eating from the forbidden fruit, the husband is at one
with her in this act (cf. 3.6, 'and she gave also to her husband
with her and he ate'). Trible notes that the man follows the
woman 'without question or comment' (p. 113). However,

with the act of disobedience and its aftermath the unity of the male and the female is disrupted. Trible shows that there are three moments in the relationship between the man and the woman; before disobedience, with(in) disobedience and after disobedience. In the first, the distinctions combined in fulfilment, in the second they became oppositions. In the third, the unity of the one flesh is shattered. 'The man turns against the woman whom he earlier recognized as bone of bone and flesh of flesh' (p. 119).

In the sentences pronounced upon the serpent, the man and the woman, the woman is the only one who is not cursed. Yet the outcome is bad for her. Commenting on 3.16—'Your desire shall be for your husband, and he shall rule over you'—Trible says that the woman desires the original unity between male and female but that the man will not reciprocate. He wishes to rule over her, and in so doing corrupts himself and his wife:

> His supremacy is neither a divine right nor a male prerogative. Her subordination is neither a divine decree nor the female destiny. Both their positions result from shared disobedience. God describes this consequence but does not prescribe it as punishment (p. 128).

However, the man complicates the matter by giving his wife a name (3.20), an act that recalls his assumption of power over the animals by giving them names. The woman is, in effect, reduced to the status of an animal:

> The act itself faults the man for corrupting one flesh of equality, for asserting power over the woman, and for violating the companion corresponding to him (p. 133).

This sketch of Trible's treatment of Genesis 2–3 has concentrated only on her interpretation of texts which have been used to maintain male supremacy, and has omitted much in her treatment which is illuminating. Something that must not be overlooked is her discussion of the relation between the earth-creature and the rest of the created order prior to the disobedience. The earth-creature was placed in a garden in which grew 'every tree which is pleasant to the sight and good for food' (2.9). The world of nature thus provided pleasure for the earth-creature at the level of sight and taste. In return, the earth-creature looked after the garden, preserving its order and beauty. Thus work was a joyful unity between the earth-creature and nature:

> Distinction without opposition, dominion without domination, hierarchy without oppression: to serve and to keep the garden is to live life in harmony and pleasure (pp. 85-86).

At the same time, the command not to eat of a certain tree showed that freedom, within limits, was assigned to the earth-creature, and it also showed that there were limits to human dominion. 'Nature itself also has God-given independence' (p. 87).

The creation of the animals increases the dominion of the earth-creature. Although they, like it, are formed from the ground, its dominion over them is indicated when it gives them names. God is the 'generous delegator of power who even forfeits the right to reverse human decisions [to give whatever name is appropriate]' (p. 93). The animals do not satisfy the earth-creature (this is God's viewpoint), and their creation paves the way for the creation of the companion and the disobedience that results.

Whether or not we are convinced by Trible's reading it can be said, without reservation, that our appreciation of Genesis 2–3 would be very much the poorer without it.

The chapters by Myers (1988) on Genesis 2–3 acknowledge the work of Trible, and occasionally draw upon her analysis. However, the methodology is quite different. Myers holds that Genesis 2–3 must be recognized as containing myth, aetiology and wisdom teaching, and must be understood from their social and historical setting in ancient Israel. She accepts that the two chapters are part of the J document for which she also accepts a tenth-century dating, and she suggests in addition that parts of the story may be even earlier. Their social setting is that of Israelite agriculture in the highlands of Canaan at the beginning of the monarchy.

In this setting, women were required to do very hard work as they helped to grow food in a far-from-helpful environment. This was a labour-intensive activity, which also involved the building and maintenance of terraces. Viewed from this standpoint of harsh reality, the position of the earth-creature in Genesis 2 was indeed to be envied. Its food came from succulent fruit trees provided by God (2.9). In 3.7-18, however ('in toil you shall eat of it [the land]...in the sweat of your face you shall eat bread...'), the text speaks of the harsh realities of agricultural life in highland Canaan; its purpose was to help the Israelite settlers there to cope with these harsh realities. Such an approach also sheds light on the incident of eating the forbidden fruit. To the people for whom Genesis 2–3 was composed, eating and providing food to eat constituted the difference between life and death. Behind the narrative of Genesis 3 are folk explanations of the human abhorrence of snakes, and of the vital connection between food (eating) and life.

Myers also devotes a chapter to Gen. 3.16, whose detailed argument about the correct translation of the verse cannot be reproduced here. With some support from some of the ancient versions she renders the verse:

> I will greatly increase your toil and your pregnancies;
> (Along) with travail shall you beget children.
> For to your man is your desire,
> and he shall predominate over you (p. 118),

and she explains the translation thus:

> Women have to work hard and have many children, as lines 1 and 2 proclaim; their reluctance to conform, which is not explicitly stated but can be reconstructed by looking at the biological and socio-economic realities of ancient Palestine, had to be overcome. Lines 3 and 4 tell us how: female reluctance is overcome by the passion they feel towards their men, and that allows them to accede to the males' sexual advances even though they realize that undesired pregnancies (with the accompanying risks) might be the consequence (p. 117).

For Myers, then, Gen. 3.16 is addressed to Israelite women living and working in the Canaanite highlands in the early Iron Age. They lived during the formative period of ancient Israel when the people had a newly acquired sense of unity and a common faith in Yahweh. Their situation demanded intense agricultural labour, together with the need to increase the population significantly. It is this combination of hard work and the need to bear many children that is apparent in 3.16, and which is given divine sanction. In interpreting the verse, Myers explicitly rejects a canonical reading of the text which would connect it with the act of disobedience in eating the fruit. 'The oracles have an independent etiological force. Hence, the prescriptions in them become penalties only in their canonical position within the prose framework' (p. 119).

Myers's exposition is an interesting use of historical-critical and ethno-archaeological work, combined with a hermeneutical approach that is similar to a hermeneutics of suspicion, without a declared intention to mistrust the text. Myers's mistrust is rather directed against the misuse of the text in its canonical form. Her treatment of the eating of the forbidden fruit prompts one to ask whether, on the view that myths justify alterations to the environmental balance and the effect these alterations have on societies, the narrative derives from a situation in which an increase in population made it necessary to prohibit the products of fruit trees for use as food. If this were so, however, the setting would hardly be the central highlands of Canaan, although the Shephelah might just be a possibility.

A quite different feminist reading of part of Genesis 1–11 is Bird's discussion of 1.26-29 (Bird 1981, pp. 129-59). Her starting point is the rift that has developed between biblical scholars and theologians with the latter, in her opinion, making pronouncements about the 'image of God' which have little or no basis in the biblical text. Bird is feminist in the sense that feminism has provided 'a new socio-theological context, characterized by new questions, perceptions and judgments' (p. 134). It is from this new perspective that she undertakes a fresh look at 1.26-30 from a traditional historical-critical standpoint. A careful examination of the use of the word for 'image' in Hebrew, and in Akkadian texts, leads to the conclusion that, in the latter, a king who is described as the image of God is designated as a special representative of the god, holding a mandate to rule on its behalf. The king so designated is divine in his function as a representative and as a ruler. Against this, Bird argues that, in 1.26, language restricted in Mesopotamia (and possibly Canaan) to the king is applied to humanity as a whole. Humanity in its essential nature stands in a special relationship to the divine world (p. 144).

The statement that God created humanity as male and female (1.27) has nothing to do with the statement that humanity was created in the divine image, according to Bird (pp. 146ff.). Its meaning is limited to the reproduction of the human race, for which both male and female were required. This reproduction will enable humanity to fill and rule the earth:

> There is no message of shared dominion here, no word about the distribution of roles, responsibility and authority between the sexes, no word of sexual equality. What is described is a task for the species... and the position of the species in relation to other orders of creation (p. 151).

Bird summarizes the results of her historical-critical search for the message/intentions of the ancient author(s) as follows: P is not an 'equal rights' theologian, nor does he suggest that the divine nature, as read back from the image, contains male and female. The words about sexual distinction refer only to the reproductive task of the human race. On the other hand, the text allows us to say that, since male and female are both human, then woman 'images the divine as fully as man and... she is consequently as essential as he to an understanding of humanity as God's special sign or representative in the world' (p. 159). Bird adds that this conclusion, while exegetically sound, probably 'exceeds what the Priestly writer intended to say or was able to conceive'.

5. Genesis 1–11 and ancient Near Eastern texts

That parts of Genesis 1–11 have much in common with the traditions of other peoples of the ancient Near East has become even clearer in the past twenty years than it already was, thanks to the publication of new texts and the publication of improved editions of already known texts. A good example is the edition of the *Atra-hasis* text by Lambert and Millard (1969). The use to which such information has been put has moved away from the attempts of earlier scholarship either to interpret the Old Testament traditions almost wholly in terms of the culture of ancient Babylon or to assert the absolute uniqueness of Israel's use of material shared with its neighbours. Arguments both for similarity with and difference from other traditions of the ancient Near East have continued to be

put forward, but in different ways and with a more moderate
tone; and more attention than before has been paid, in making
the comparisons, to material from Egypt and to ancient Near
Eastern art. In a series of studies, Müller has stressed the positive side of the similarities between parts of Genesis 1–11 and
ancient Near Eastern parallels (Müller 1972, 1985). He has
argued that what he regards as the original form of ch. 2
(vv. 4b-8, [10-14], 15b, 18-24) is mythical in the sense that the
narrative serves the same function as similar ancient Near
Eastern traditions, which is to explain and to legitimate
humanity's position in its world. Faced by forces, especially in
the world of nature, that shape and often threaten human life,
it is necessary for humanity to name these forces and to tell
stories about them in order to make the world more hospitable.
The fact that Genesis 1–11 speaks of God rather than gods
does not alter this fact. It is not the presence or absence of gods
that determines whether texts are mythical: it is their function.

All this is not original to Müller, as he readily indicates; but
he develops this view in some interesting directions. In his
study of the flood narrative (Müller, 1985), he points out that
the combination of a creation story and a flood story in a single
text is not peculiar to the Old Testament, but is found also in
Atra-hasis and in the Sumerian flood story about Ziusudra. He
believes the connection between creation and flood stories to be
important, and labels the flood story an anti-myth, a story of
the destruction of order. The two stories taken together—
creation (myth) and flood (anti-myth)—articulate an understanding of what it means to be human that is essentially
paradoxical. The texts describe a situation in which the world
is not an ordered whole but an interaction of tensions, in which
the incomplete power of God or the gods over the whole of
reality is dramatically portrayed (Müller 1985, p. 308).

From this position, Müller develops two ideas. The first is
that the world view expressed in these Old Testament and
other traditions is not the product of the thinking of isolated
individuals, but arises rather from the collective experience of
humanity, and is thus the expression of inter-subjectivity. Yet
the texts are also sufficiently open to differing uses and interpretations that they can serve as an expression of human self-

awareness in varying situations. Müller compares here the reasons given in Genesis 6 for the flood with the different reasons given in the other texts. We might add that this suggestion may explain the continuing importance of these texts even today.

Müller's second main point is that these traditions must not be explained away as being merely pre-scientific or an expression of humanity's biological needs. They are concerned with the relationship between the human and the non-human in the world, and how this relationship may be brought to expression in speech and thought. In this regard, they have much in common with modern scientific attempts to explain the world, as well as with those of Christian theology employing the mythological language of the incarnation of God. The very fact that these traditions are not peculiar to the Bible, but can be shown to be an expression of human subjectivity, is a reminder to theology that its ultimate task is to understand reality and to do this in dialogue with other scientific disciplines. Thus Müller skilfully uses the similarities between parts of Genesis 1–11 and ancient Near Eastern texts in order to give the passages an almost timeless, existential significance.

The opposite approach has been to contrast Genesis 1–11 and the parallel traditions by showing how Genesis 1–11 has used motifs common to these texts in distinctive ways. Thus Bird (1981), in discussing humankind's creation in the image of God, refers to Egyptian evidence 'where the idea of the king as image of the god is a common one, finding expression in a rich and diverse vocabulary of representation which describes the Pharaoh as image, statue, likeness, picture, etc., of the deity (usually the chief creator god)' (p. 140). She also refers to similar evidence from Mesopotamia which is closer to P in language, conception and time, before going on to argue that Genesis 1 is unique in using the image language to describe not a king, but humanity as a whole in relation to God.

Other approaches along these lines are as follows. In some texts from the ancient Near East, human beings are created by the gods to perform the hard labour that the gods do not wish to do. In Genesis 2, the man (or earth-creature) is created to tend the garden; but his/its function is not to toil, and food is abundantly provided from fruit trees. When toil becomes the lot of humanity, this is because of human disobedience, not divine arbitrariness. Again, in some texts, humanity is created from the blood of the gods. In Genesis 2, the part of humanity that comes from God is the breath; thus the difference between God and humanity is emphasized. Genesis 1–2 is unique in ancient Near Eastern texts so far known to us in describing the creation of women (see Rogerson and Davies, 1989, pp. 198-208 for the above paragraph).

Zenger, in his monograph on the Priestly parts of Genesis 1–11, makes use of the rich material assembled from ancient Near Eastern art by Othmar Keel, regarding the bow, and the relation between human beings and animals. He also cites an Egyptian text from about the fifteenth century BCE, the myth of the heavenly cow. This describes a time when there was harmony in the created order between the gods and humankind. This was disrupted, however, by a rebellion of the humans, caused by the ageing of the creator god Re. This ideal world could not continue in unaltered existence, but was subject to decay followed by regeneration. The rebellion of humankind was punished by the creator god by a fire supervised by the goddess Hathor. However, the creator god himself rescued some human beings, and inaugurated a new order far less satisfactory than the former situation. The only access to the former creation is through death, and the creator god effectively withdraws from human affairs.

This story contains some motifs also found in Genesis 1–11. An ideal creation is disrupted by human rebellion against the god, there is a destruction (by fire, not water) and another order emerges, falling short of the original creation. The differences are also striking compared with Genesis 1–11. As Zenger puts it:

> P^g begins with the concept of a complete creation which, left to take care of itself, becomes a corrupted world full of violence. This does not lead, however, to the disappointed withdrawal of the Creator God, but to the acknowledgment of his active involvement by means of the 'sign of the cloud', which indicates his residence not in a remote heavenly palace, but among his people (p. 134).

Comparison with ancient Near Eastern texts, therefore, continues to be a fruitful part of the study of Genesis 1–11, but with new emphases.

6. Discussion and evaluation

Faced with the great variety of approaches and conclusions that have been mentioned in this chapter, readers can be forgiven for feeling bewildered. They may find themselves thinking that however interesting many of the individual insights of these approaches may be, they surely cannot all be correct or equally valid, and that means that we have no certain way of discovering what Genesis 1–11 is saying.

In reply to this natural reaction we can say that the history of interpretation shows that there probably never has been a time when all interpreters were agreed about the meaning of Genesis 1–11, and that each generation of interpreters has been influenced by what they have found in the text in relation to the situation in which they worked (for some examples see Rogerson, 1988). If the present state of affairs is different from what previously was the case, it is a difference of degree. The diversity of modern readings of Genesis 1–11 arises from a greater diversity of situations in which the text is being read. Yet, as will be argued, this greater diversity can be reduced to an underlying unity. This will not mean that we shall then get an agreed answer to the question, 'What is Genesis 1–11 saying?' It will mean that we shall be in a better position to understand the reasons why we are studying the text and what it is that we want from it. This self-discovery will assist each of us as we study Genesis 1–11. Underlying all of the approaches outlined in this chapter is a decision or decisions taken by the interpreters either deliberately or unawares. These will now be stated and discussed, but not in any particular order of importance.

a. *Sources versus final form*
This book will not argue for or against dividing Genesis 1–11 into the sources J and P. In Chapter 3 below, some sections will give reasons why certain parts of Genesis 1–11 have been divided into sources, and there will also be references to litera-

ture that advocates or rejects source division. The task here will simply be to discuss the implications of choosing or rejecting the sources theory in interpreting Genesis 1–11.

The first issue that arises is whether the Bible is to be interpreted as a whole (although this is not as simple as it seems, as will be explained) or whether certain traditions are to be set over against other traditions. The setting of traditions in opposition is most clearly seen in the work of Lohfink, where P^g is held to be giving a different view of the meaning of Israelite history compared with J or D. Myers sets traditions in opposition in a slightly different way when she interprets Gen. 3.16 in its presumed historical and sociological context, and deliberately rejects the link between this passage and the act of disobedience in ch. 3. As I understand her, she is rejecting a reading of 3.16 that the final form of the text makes possible, and is opposing to that reading an interpreting of 3.16 regarded as an original, isolated unit.

It must be stressed that putting traditions in opposition is not a necessary consequence of accepting source criticism or of breaking the sources into smaller, prior units. It is possible to accept the existence of the distinct sources J and P and nevertheless to interpret them harmoniously. One can argue, for example, that it was the P writer who composed Genesis 1–11 by incorporating J into his own account, and who thereby stamped his own intentionality upon the whole, regardless of what the J material might have meant in isolation.

Readings of the final form of Genesis 1–11 are of various types. They can be literary, structuralist or historical-critical. An excellent example of the first type is that of Clines. He decides to make no attempt to appeal to sources or to historical background (although he discusses these matters carefully) in his attempt to find a 'theme' that will do the greatest possible justice to the literary features of Genesis 1–11. No structuralist reading of the text as a whole was discussed in this chapter, but such a reading would eschew sources (though not necessarily historical setting) in an attempt to detect beneath the literary surface of the text various oppositions or distinctions that suggest themselves as part of the underlying structure. An historical-critical reading of the final form of Genesis 1–11, such as would be implied in the canonical approach of Childs

(Childs, pp. 148-50), would not reject the existence of sources nor rule out a long process of composition. It would, nevertheless, maintain that however Genesis 1–11 reached its final form, and whatever may have been the sources used, the final form has an intentionality that scholarship must try to discover by historical-critical rather than by formal literary methods.

It is possible to combine some of the underlying decisions mentioned above. There is no reason why a scholar should not accept J and P, accept that, in isolation, they express different ideologies, and yet also accept that, in combining them, their redactor or editor understood them as expressing yet a third viewpoint. This, however, raises the issue that is discussed in the next section. In a case such as that immediately above, where a scholar is accepting three intentionalities of Genesis 1–11—that of J, that of P, and that of the editor—is one of these to be preferred as more 'authoritative'? This issue does not arise, of course, for those who reject sources; and one reason why some scholars reject sources may be that it relieves them from precisely this question.

b. *Intentions, motives and authority*
Brett (1990) has recently suggested that we should distinguish between intentions and motives when we interpret texts. By an intention he means that which we can infer from a text itself about what it is trying to convey. By a motive he means a judgment, based on considerations other than the text itself, about the reason why a text was written. An example of intention would be the significance of Gen. 1.26-30 and 9.1-3, (4-6), 7. The similarities and differences between these texts are the major clue to what they are seeking to convey. An example of motive would be Wittenberg's claim that the purpose of the J material was to oppose the political and social effects of the reign of Solomon. There is nothing in the text itself to suggest this, and Wittenberg bases his claim upon other considerations such as his view of the date of J and the circles that produced it.

Brett also uses the term 'indirect intention'. By this he means the interpretation of a text against the background of other texts, such as those from the ancient Near East. There is no direct evidence in Genesis 1–11 that these chapters are

referring to creation and flood stories known from ancient
Mesopotamia, or to Egyptian and Assyrian notions of the king
as the image of the god. However, there is no doubt that certain
parts of Genesis 1–11 appear to us in a new light if we assume
that their writer(s) knew some or all of these extra-biblical
traditions.

Brett's suggestions enable us to distinguish between three
types of operation, although it can be conceded that, in practice, they may merge and overlap. First, there is the attempt to
establish from the text itself what it is trying to convey. Second,
there is the study of the text primarily from the point of view of
its motivation within a presumed political and social setting.
Third, there is an attempt to put the text in the wider context
of ideas known from extra-biblical material to have existed in
the ancient Near East.

Even if some of these operations overlap, a weighting
towards one or the other may produce differing interpretations. For example, Bird comes to a different conclusion from
Beauchamp about the meaning of humankind's creation in
the divine image. This is because she interprets 1.26ff. partly in
the light of Egyptian and Assyrian texts, whereas Beauchamp
is concerned to work out the exegetical problems provoked by
the contrast between Gen. 1.26-30 and 9.1-7. Again, Boesak's
reading of Genesis 4 plays very close attention to the text of
that chapter and the meaning suggested by its literary features, whereas Mosala's interpretation of the same passage is
far from obvious because he is concerned with the motives
behind the text's production.

What is the 'authority' of these various decisions and their
resulting interpretations? Strictly speaking, this is a religious
question generated by the fact that Christians have believed
that the Bible is in some sense a communication from God to
humanity—a proposition to which the present author is
committed. But can a text be a communication from God if a
diversity of ways of reading it gives rise to so many interpretations? The same difficulty may be felt by non-believers who
expect, perhaps without having asked themselves why, that
Genesis 1–11 should have at least one interpretation that can
be regarded as 'authoritative'.

In an attempt to resolve these matters several strategies could be employed. It could be argued, for example, that a reading is more likely to be 'authoritative' if it eliminates uncertainties. For example, the final form of the text exists, whereas the discerning of sources is theoretical. Again, suggestions about the motivation of the writer(s) are theoretical, since we actually know so little about how and when the texts were produced. Again, we do not actually know whether the writer(s) of Genesis 1–11 were familiar with other creation and flood stories from the ancient world. The result of this kind of argument would be that an interpretation whose aim was to discover the intentionality of the final form of Genesis 1–11 from the inner dynamics of the text was more 'authoritative' than readings which resulted from assumptions that were no more than plausible.

This kind of argument is given only as an example; and it is not the purpose of this guide either to reject or to endorse it. It must also be stated that there are scholars who are absolutely convinced that the only way to discover the meaning of the text is to isolate the sources of which it is believed to be composed and to see how these sources have been used in the final composition.

Another crucial question that has to be addressed is that of the relationship between the meaning of a text and what we take to be its intentionality or motive. The meaning cannot be confined to intentionality or motive, from which it follows that 'authority' cannot be confined to intentionality or motive either. This can be illustrated as follows. According to Wittenberg, the motive for writing Genesis 11 was to criticize the building schemes of Solomon. Let us assume that he is correct. Does it follow from this that any other interpretation of the tower of Babel story is incorrect, or to be ruled out? Are we wrong to see it as a story of humankind in general, wrongly and vainly trying to enter those realms that probably belong to God alone? Surely not. Again (and this is a personal view) I doubt very much that the writer of Genesis 2 thought that the 'ādām that God placed in the garden of Eden was an earth-creature that was neither male nor female. This does not mean, however, that I reject out of hand Trible's reading of this passage in those terms. On the contrary, she has enriched these chapters by the suggestions that she has made. This brings me to the point where I must try to state what I believe to be a unity underlying the diversities that have been outlined in this chapter. It can be summarized in the following statement: What is common to all these approaches is that they are the work of interpretative communities and that these communities have an implicit view of what it means to be a human being.

At the end of the nineteenth century, the churches and universities and colleges constituted a single interpretative community, whose main concern was to answer the questions arising from the natural sciences, especially Darwinism. The implied view of what it means to be human was that humans were essentially thinking creatures whose intellectual questions needed to be answered. The twentieth century saw a growing apart of the churches and the universities. The need to understand Genesis 1–11 in the light of newly discovered Babylonian texts was an academic rather than an ecclesiastical concern. What has happened in the past twenty years is that there has been an increase in the number of interpretative communities, and that some of these have become established within universities.

The most obvious new interpretative communities have been those concerned with liberation and feminism. It will be clear from what was said earlier in the chapter that liberation and feminist standpoints can vary and even disagree among themselves. What is distinctive about liberation interpretative communities, however, is that they do not view human beings as simply thinking creatures with primarily intellectual concerns. Human beings are social beings embedded in political and economic structures; and where these structures oppress, discriminate and de-humanize, they must be resisted. In such situations the biblical text becomes a partner in the struggle to achieve conditions worthy of the dignity which belongs to human beings.

Similar things can be said about feminist interpretative communities. Their concern is to make the biblical text a partner in the struggle against sexism, so that a new and appropriate understanding can emerge of the respective contributions of males and females to the business of living as human beings.

In academic circles twenty years ago there was probably still only one principal interpretative community, even though its interests were many and varied. This was the community that believed in study for its own sake, and which therefore implicitly understood humans to be essentially thinking and rational creatures. The situation today in academic circles is that, increasingly, there is a willingness to entertain the possibility of other interpretative communities having a legitimate place alongside that which believes in study for its own sake. This chapter has indicated the results of this new diversity. Of course, what I have just written gives too rigid a picture, as though people belong to different interpretative communities that exist in watertight compartments. In fact, many people belong to more than one such community. It is possible, for example, for an individual to be committed to one of the churches, to work in a university and to be a feminist. But it is also likely that one of these interpretative communities will be considered to be the most important, and will influence that person's work more strongly than the rest.

It is within the interpretative communities that the standards for acceptable readings are established. If the main interpretative community is a church, that body's beliefs and concepts of mission will ultimately decide what is and is not an acceptable reading of Genesis 1–11. For example, a church that is doctrinally committed to the subordinate role of women is not likely to approve of interpretations that seek to establish female equality with males. If the main interpretative community is a university, sympathy with other approaches will be difficult to obtain if their readings of Genesis 1–11 rely on impossible translations of the Hebrew or implausible reconstructions of the social and historical background to the text. If the main interpretative community is one actively engaged in the struggle against injustice, there will probably be little enthusiasm for readings of Genesis 1–11 that are mainly interested in relating the flood story to the *Atra-hasis* narrative.

All this implies that, as well as taking the academic decisions mentioned earlier, such as opting for the final form as against interpreting J and P, readers need to reflect upon their membership of interpretative communities and what are the considerations that are the most influential in determining how they prefer to interpret Genesis 1–11. It is very much to be hoped that members of differing interpretative communities will be prepared to listen to each other and to learn from each other. The current great diversity of approaches to reading Genesis 1–11 should be seen not as a threat but as an opportunity. They all represent the activity of that human race whose origins and nature are the subject of Genesis 1–11.

One final consideration is that, as time progresses, some readings of texts stand the test of time, whereas others are quickly forgotten. This will surely be the case with regard to some of the interpretations discussed in this chapter. At the same time, the history of interpretation shows that in every generation, differing interpretations are part of a continuing struggle to hear the text of the Bible addressing communities as the Word of God. Even if there are many voices, and they sound confusing, their existence is a testimony to the fact that the biblical text is alive and not simply a dead letter.

3

CRITICAL
ISSUES

1. Myth

A T VARIOUS TIMES in the past two hundred years, and for various reasons, it has been suggested that parts or all of Genesis 1–11 are myths or mythical (see Rogerson, 1974 for an extensive survey). Two separate questions will be dealt with here: How did the presumed Israelite readers of Genesis 1–11 understand these passages? What do we mean when we classify Genesis 1–11 or parts thereof as myths or mythical?

There can be no doubt that when Israelites read Genesis 1–11 they believed that these stories belonged to an age that was different from their own times. Yet this past age was in continuity with their own times, and what had happened then determined what the world was like now. We find in Genesis 1–11 a series of phrases which mark off the narratives as belonging to a different age. They are:

1.1   When God began to create (if this is the correct rendering; see below, §2).
2.4b   In the day that the Lord made the earth and the heavens...
2.25   and the man and his wife were both naked and were not ashamed...
3.1   now the serpent was more subtle...
6.1   When men began to multiply on the face of the ground...
6.4   Nephilim (giants) were on the earth in those days.
11.1   Now the whole earth had one language and few words...

Müller (1972, p. 265 n. 22) gives some parallels from the ancient world. To these phrases must be added the fact that ancient Israelites did not expect snakes to speak (in Hebrew?)

or to propel themselves in an upright position, did not expect people to live to be over 900 years, and were aware that Hebrew was only one of a number of languages spoken in the ancient Near East.

We must also not overlook the fact that the narratives themselves clearly describe 'before' and 'after' situations, making it explicitly clear that there can be no return to the 'before' situations. Thus, humanity is forever banished from the garden of Eden, and the earth is no longer benign when it comes to producing food. The possibility is excluded that there will ever again be a flood that totally destroys the earth and its inhabitants. Humankind remains separated by the barriers of language.

On the other hand, the age that is described by Genesis 1–11 has continuity with that of the Israelite readers. This is indicated by the genealogies that form a chain of descendants from Adam to Abraham: ten generations from Adam to Noah and ten from Noah to Abraham, with the first series characterized by the very long ages lived by the men of those generations. Other links are provided by the explanations (aetiologies) that begin from the world as known by the Israelite readers and refer back to the world of Genesis 1–11 as though to say: you know that the stories of this past age are true because of what is true in your own world. For example, the fact that when a man and a woman marry they enter into a deeper relationship than they had with their parents (2.24) indicates the truth of the story of the woman being first made from the man's rib. Again, the fact that a rainbow appears in the sky only when it has been raining is a confirmation of the story that the world was once destroyed by a flood (van Dyck, 1990).

For Israelites, then, the narratives of Genesis 1–11 were factually true, but Israelites did not expect to experience the things that they describe. Adam and Eve were accepted as real human beings, but any Israelite woman who claimed that she had had a conversation with a snake would have been dismissed as a crank. The stories in Genesis 1–11, compiled from ancient traditions about origins which the Israelite shared with other ancient Near Eastern peoples, and enriched with folk tale motifs (see Rogerson 1978, pp. 66-85), expressed Israel's understanding of how the world of their experience had been brought into being by the God of Israel, and how it had been shaped by the response of their forefathers.

So far, we have been considering what the narratives meant to the Israelites. A quite different matter arises when we today designate Genesis 1–11 as myth. We are using a classification which is based upon the comparative study of the literatures of ancient and modern underdeveloped peoples. Although the terms 'myths' and 'mythical' have been used in many ways, three can be selected for brief mention. The first is a literary definition of 'myths' which goes back to the work of the brothers J. and W. Grimm in the nineteenth century (Rogerson 1974, pp. 27-28). According to this view, myths are stories about the gods, from which it has often been concluded, rightly or wrongly, that Genesis 1–11 contains no myths except, perhaps, for 6.4, where the 'sons of God' marry human wives. Another view, which became widespread in the present century, is the ritual theory of myth, according to which myths are the liturgies that accompany rituals. On the face of it, this removes Genesis 1–11 from the category of myth since we have no evidence that any of its material was used in ritual; and in any case the ritual theory itself has been largely rejected (Rogerson, 1974, pp. 66-84). The third view is that of Müller, mentioned in Chapter 2. Müller has argued convincingly that, with regard to their general function in articulating an understanding of the world, the narratives of Genesis 1–11 cannot be treated differently from similar traditions from the ancient Near East, even if the latter are polytheistic and Genesis is monotheistic. Müller's view has the advantage of linking Genesis 1–11 with similar ancient material, and of seeing it as a fundamental expression of the human striving to discover truth, while leaving open the need to interpret the actual content of Genesis 1–11 in its own terms. Müller's approach to myth is, in my view, the best option for modern interpretation of Genesis 1–11.

2. Genesis 1.1-3

A glance at recent translations of the Bible indicates that the rendering of the opening of Genesis is not without problems. The RSV opens with 'In the beginning God created' but has a small (a) after 'created' and a footnote giving as an alternative translation 'When God began to create...' The NEB has something like the RSV footnote as its main text, with the traditional words relegated to a footnote. In the REB the situation found in the RSV has been restored.

The main problem is that in the traditional vocalized Hebrew text, the phrase $b^e r\bar{e}\check{s}\hat{\imath}t$ (traditionally rendered as 'In the beginning'), means either 'in a beginning' or, if it is to be translated 'in the beginning' it must introduce a subordinate clause such as 'of God's creating...' Unfortunately, the immediately following words in the traditional vocalized Hebrew text cannot be rendered 'of God's creating'. Therefore both the traditional translation, 'In the beginning God created', and the alternative, 'When God began to create', imply an alteration to the vocalization of the Hebrew. The former implies reading $b\bar{a}r\bar{e}\check{s}\hat{\imath}t$ for $b^a r\bar{e}\check{s}\hat{\imath}t$ and the second implies reading $b^e r\bar{o}$' (infinitive construct) for $b\bar{a}r\bar{a}$' (3rd masculine singular perfect). These and other problems have led to three main suggestions about the translation of the syntax of 1.1-3.

> (1) The traditional translation in which each of verses 1, 2 and 3 is a statement:
>> In the beginning God created the heavens and the earth (v. 1).
>> The earth was without form and void (v. 2).
>> And God said, 'Let there be light' (v. 3).
> (2) The rendering 'When God began to create the heavens and the earth, the earth was without form and void... Then God said, "Let there be light..." '
> (3) The rendering 'When God began to create the heavens and the earth—now the earth was without form and void...—God said, "Let there be light..." '

In trying to decide between these alternatives, one view must be rejected, namely that which prefers (1) on the ground that it implies the doctrine that God created the world out of nothing (*creatio ex nihilo*), whereas (2) and (3) imply creation out of pre-existing matter. For a careful look at (1) will indicate that it, too, implies creation out of pre-existing matter. In Genesis 1 the creative acts result from the divine word, 'And God said...' Gen. 1.1 is a statement and not a creative word, and it is followed by the information that 'The earth was without form and void'. Since order and ordering are an essential part of the Old Testament view of creation (see below), the earth had not been created if it was 'without form and void'. It was an undifferentiated mass waiting to be formed into shape.

A stronger argument in favour of (1) is that, whereas v. 1 says that God created the heavens, there is no mention of the creation of the heavens later in the passage (in v. 2). Gen. 1.1 is probably to be understood as follows: 'In the beginning God created the heavens and the earth'. This is a summary statement of what God had done, in which no elaboration is needed of how he brought into being the heavens, which are his own abode. The earth that had been brought into being was, however, an undifferentiated mass, and the purpose of the remainder of the chapter is to describe how this was ordered into a whole for the prime benefit of humankind among the created things.

In v. 2 the words 'without form and void', 'darkness', and 'deep' suggest something sinister about the unformed earth and its waters, and this has led scholars to compare this verse with descriptions of chaos prior to creation in ancient Near Eastern texts (cf. *ANET*, pp. 60-61). The Hebrew word for 'deep', *t^ehôm*, has been compared with the name of the goddess Tiamat, out of whose carcass the victorious god Marduk made the world in the Babylonian epic of creation, *Enuma elish* (*ANET*, p. 67), although philologically the two words cannot be connected. It has further been maintained that the phrase translated in the RSV as 'The Spirit of God was moving over the face of the waters' should be rendered as 'a mighty wind was swirling across the face of the waters'. This would mean that the phrase was a description of chaos prior to creation and nothing to do with the Spirit of God.

These are difficult questions to decide. We do not know whether the writer of Genesis 1 was familiar with other creation stories or their motifs or whether, if he was, how he intended references to them in his text to be taken (if there were such references). It is probably unwise to look for allusions to other ancient Near Eastern texts or motifs in order to provide the clue to the understanding of these verses. If Gen. 1.1 asserts that God created the heavens and the earth it is most likely that the phrase about the Spirit of God should be understood in its traditional sense. Thus, although there may be something sinister about the as yet unordered earth, even this is under the divine influence as the Spirit of God hovers bird-like (cf. Deut. 32.11) over the unformed matter.

3. 'Word' and 'deed' accounts and the translation of Genesis 1

In Genesis 1, two types of creative activity can be found: creation by word and creation by deed. An example of the former is 1.3, 'Let there be light', and an example of the latter is 1.7, 'God made the firmament'. However, in the case of the creation of the firmament we also have the words, 'God said, "Let there be a firmament..."' (v. 6). Does this imply that the firmament is created twice, once by word and once by deed? This possible double creation led Schmidt (1967[2]) to argue in an influential monograph that Genesis 1 in its final form was a combination of two accounts, a word account and a deed account. This view has since been challenged by Steck (1981[2]). The most important thing about the discussion, however, is how it affects the translation of Genesis 1. The view that there is a word account and a deed account depends partly on a particular understanding of the phrase 'And it was so' in vv. 9, 11, 15 and 24. If we take vv. 24-25 we seem to have the following elements:

Word account

> 24 God said 'Let the earth bring forth living creatures...'
> And it was so (i.e. it happened in accordance with God's command).

Deed account

> 25 God made the beasts of the earth.

However, it is possible to render vv. 24-25 as follows:

> 24 God said, 'The earth shall bring forth living creatures...'
> And it was so (i.e. in accordance with what God had said):
> 25 God made the beasts of the earth.

On this view the 'Let there be' statements in vv. 6, 9 not in the Hebrew text, but in the ancient Greek translation known as the Septuagint or LXX), 14, 20 and 24 are not words that create, but statements that declare how God intends the world to be ordered. These declarations are then put into effect by God. In fact, a translation such as the RSV could be read in the way that is being suggested here. In vv. 14-19, for example, the words 'Let there be light in the firmament of the heavens' can be read as a declaration of intent, and the words in v. 16, 'God made the two great lights...', can be regarded as the actual creation. The GNB on the other hand, goes a long way towards supporting the word and deed accounts theory by rendering 'And it was so' as 'So it was done'.

If we pursue the matter further, we notice some interesting variations in the structure of the accounts in Genesis 1.

(1) Creation of light (v. 3)
God said...
(no 'it was so')
(no 'God created the light')

(2) Creation of the firmament (vv. 6-7)
God said...
God made the firmament
'It was so' (*after* God made the firmament!)

(3) Creation of the dry land (v. 9)
God said...
It was so
(no 'God made'—but this is found in the LXX)

(4) Creation of plants and trees (vv. 11-12)
God said...
It was so
The earth brought forth

(5) Creation of luminaries (vv. 14-16)
God said...
It was so
God made...

(6) Creation of sea creatures and birds (vv. 20-21)
God said...
(no 'It was so')
God made

(7) Creation of beasts of the earth (vv. 24-25)
God said...
It was so
God made

(8) Creation of human beings (vv. 26-27)
God said

(no 'It was so')
God made...

This indicates that the pattern

God said
It was so
God made...

occurs only twice, for acts (5) and (7), and three times if we include (3). (4) is close to the formula, except that it is the earth that produces the plants and trees, and not God that makes them. Indeed, (4) seems to be evidence against a separate 'word' account and to support the view that 'Let there be' is a declaration of intended order:

God said, 'The earth shall put forth vegetation...' It happened (in accordance with God's command): The earth brought forth vegetation...

If this approach is correct, then we need to understand the 'Let there be' statements in Genesis 1 to refer not only to what God meant to happen at creation: we need to understand them as statements laying down an eternal ordering of the world, an ordering that was begun at creation and which the biblical writer believed to endure to his own day.

4. The creation as 'good'

A recurrent feature of Genesis 1 is the statement 'God saw that it was good'. This occurs in vv. 9, 12, 18, 21 and 25. It is not found in vv. 6-8 (the creation of the firmament) and in v. 4 there is the variant 'God saw that the light was good'. At v. 31 this motif is summed up 'God saw everything that he had made, and behold it was very good'. This is clearly an important motif. What does it mean?

One often hears it said, on the basis of Genesis 1, that the created order is good in the sense of being a perfect expression of God's will. This must, however, be regarded as dubious. Even if this is what Genesis 1 means, we cannot ignore the cursing of the ground in Genesis 3 (if we are doing a final form reading) nor the qualification of 1.26-30 in 9.1-7 following the flood (if we are reading the final form or interpreting P^g).

These passages indicate that the creation as it was in Genesis 1 no longer exists in the precise form that it did then. This is further borne out by passages such as Isa. 11.6-9 and 65.17-25 in which a new creation is envisaged in which there is no enmity between humans and animals nor between animals and animals.

Zenger (pp. 59-62) has an interesting discussion of the matter on the basis of which it could be suggested that by 'good' the passage means 'good for achieving its purpose'. The structure of most of the works of creation will then be:

Declaration of intent: Let there be . . .
Creative work: God made . . .
Acknowledgment: that what has been made meets the intention. God saw that it was good.

This understanding of 'good' in a weakened sense then enables us to say that, in spite of the curse, the flood and the compromise (9.1-7), the creation is still 'good' in that it provides the order and stability in which the life given by God can be lived out. It is doubtful whether the creation any longer expresses the ideal will of God; but this does not rule out its 'goodness' as providing a viable setting for human and animal life.

5. Creation as order

The previous section leads on to the idea of creation as order, in that it has been suggested that the description of the creation as 'good' means that it achieves its purpose of providing a stable and viable setting for human life. The idea of creation as order can be paralleled from outside Israel in the ancient world (see Schmid in Anderson 1984, pp. 102-17), and it can also be illustrated from the Old Testament itself, and with some important consequences.

In Genesis 1, the process of creation involves distinguishing, setting boundaries and assigning positions. Light is distinguished from darkness (v. 4), waters above the firmament are distinguished from those below it (v. 7), water is distinguished from dry land (v. 10), and luminaries distinguish day from night (vv. 14-15). The firmament sets a boundary between the upper and lower waters (v. 6), and the luminaries set the limits to days, nights, seasons and years (vv. 14-15). To the earth are assigned trees, plants and living creatures, to the heavens are assigned birds, and to the waters are assigned the sea and water creatures.

What is implicit in Genesis 1 is more explicitly stated elsewhere. Thus in Gen. 6.11, the flood is brought about when the waters above the firmament and the waters below the earth and the seas are allowed to burst their bounds, and to cover the whole earth. The bounds, or boundaries, receive an even more explicit mention in Job 38.8-11:

> Who shut in the sea with doors, when it burst forth from the womb,... and [I] prescribed bounds for it, and set bars and doors, and said, 'Thus far shall you come and no further...'?

Indeed, the book of Job has some charming touches when it comes to the idea of creation as order. It suggests (in poetry, of course) that there are storehouses where God keeps the snow and the hail (38.22) and that even light and darkness have their appropriate storage areas (38.19, 24).

There is an important link between creation as order and human moral behaviour, such that the latter can affect the former. This is clear from Genesis 1–11 itself. It is human disobedience that leads to the cursing of the ground (3.17-19), and human wickedness that makes God decide to bring about the flood. But there are other passages in the Old Testament that address this theme. An example is Leviticus 26 where the Israelites are promised that

> If you walk in my statutes and observe my commandments to do them, then I will give you your rains in their season, and the land shall yield its increase, and the trees of the field shall yield their fruit (Lev. 26.3-4).

The opposite is that

> if you will not hearken to me... your strength shall be spent in vain, for your land shall not yield its increase, and the trees of the field shall not yield their fruit (vv. 14, 20).

The connection between obeying God and being prosperous will strike many modern readers as naive, and certainly out of keeping with the New Testament paradox that the first followers of Jesus were called to self-denial and suffering. Others

might see here a justification for supporting ecology move-
ments, pointing out that human exploitation of natural
resources (i.e. disobeying God) does eventually lead to economic disasters. However, the most important point is the following: if creation implies order, then that order is not
restricted simply to the non-human world. If creation is order,
that order must include ordered human relationships; and if
God only guaranteed the stability of the physical universe, but
was unconcerned about inter-human relationships, then the
creation would be fundamentally immoral. The same would
be true of any form of religion that emphasized the spiritual
attainments of the individual while remaining indifferent to
disordered human relationships resulting from the evil
structures of oppression, poverty and injustice.

6. One creation story or two?

On the basis of source division, it is often asserted that there
are two accounts of creation, one in Gen. 1.1–2.4a, the other in
2.4b-25. Opponents of source division labour to deny this,
sometimes rendering the Hebrew verbs in 2.21 as pluperfects

The LORD God had caused a deep sleep to fall upon the man...

to avoid the idea that 2.21ff. is an account of the creation of
woman distinct from that implied in 1.27.

There can be no doubt that there are duplications between
Genesis 1 and 2. In the former, human beings are made at
vv. 26-30, while at 2.5 humanity does not yet exist and a man
is made in 2.7. Again, 2.19 implies, against ch. 1, that the beasts
of the field or birds of the air do not yet exist. On the other hand,
the following differences between the two chapters are
significant. In ch. 2 there is no explicit account of the creation
of light, darkness, day, night, sun, moon, stars or firmament.
There is also a detailed account, not found in ch. 1, of the loca-
tion of the Garden of Eden and of the rivers which flowed from
it (vv. 8-14). On the basis of the content of 1.1–2.4a and 2.4b-25
it is safest to say that the former is a creation story and that the
latter is an origins story. Genesis 1 relates the formation and
ordering of the universe, while Genesis 2 presumes the exis-

tence of the earth and describes how it was populated and ordered.

7. One tree or two?

It is usually held that Gen. 1.1-4a and 2.4b–3.24 come from different sources, because of the contrasting style and language of these chapters and the fact that they use different names for God. In 1.1–2.4a the Hebrew term for God is *ᵉlōhîm* while in 2.4b–3.25 it is *yhwh' ᵉlōhîm*. These are represented respectively in English translations as 'God' and 'LORD God'. However, some interpreters also find within 2.4b–3.25 itself an earlier story in which there was no mention of the tree of the knowledge of good and evil. According to this view, ch. 2 was an account of the creation of humankind and animals, now contained in 2.4b-8, 15bβ ('to till the ground and keep it') and 18-24. 2.10-14 may have been part of this account or may have been added later. But in order to link ch. 2 and 3 it was necessary for an editor to add to ch. 2 the following verses: 9, 15a, and 15bα (up to 'Garden of Eden'), 16-17 and 25.

In ch. 3, vv. 22-24 create a problem in that Adam and Eve are driven from the garden not because they disobeyed the command to eat from the tree of the knowledge of good and evil (compare 2.16-17 where only the eating of the fruit of the tree of the knowledge of good and evil is forbidden) but in order to prevent them from eating the fruit of the tree of life (3.22). There is the further problem that in 3.3 it is the tree in the midst of the garden that is prohibited, and in 2.9 that tree is the tree of life. What the humans eat is the fruit of the tree of the knowledge of good and evil. This leads to the further suggestion that, in its original form, Genesis 3 was not set in a special garden from which the offenders were then expelled. The expulsion theme, and with it the existence of the tree of life, was a literary device needed to link the original form of ch. 2 to 3.1-21. Thus the following stages of the growth of 2.4b–3.24 have been suggested:

1. There first existed two separate stories:
   (a) 2.4b-8, (10-14), 15bβ, 18-24
   (b) 3.1-21

2. The stories were linked by adding to ch. 2 the verses 15a, 15bα-17 and 25. These provided a context for 3.3 ('you shall not eat of the fruit of the tree which is in the midst of the garden') and for 3.7 ('they knew that they were naked').
3. The theme of the expulsion from Eden was introduced by the addition of 2.9 and 3.22-24, which mention the tree of life.

It is not maintained here that there were necessarily three separate stages, nor is it being denied that these suggestions are simply theories, and that is it possible to account for the paradoxes of the narrative on the hypothesis of a single author narrating a story without using pre-existing traditions. The chief value of the exercise is in alerting readers to elements in the text. For readers who are convinced by the analysis, it has the value of helping them to compare the suggested 'original' stories with other ancient traditions.

8. Genesis 3 and Ezekiel 28.11-19

The closest parallel to Genesis 3 in ancient literature comes from Ezek. 28.11-19. Although this passage is an oracle against the king and city of Tyre, it has the following similarities with Genesis 3:

1. The chief actor is placed in the Garden of Eden (v. 13).
2. He was originally perfect but later found to have iniquity (v. 15).
3. He was driven from the divine mountain by a guardian cherub.

There are also differences, in that Genesis 3 does not mention a holy mountain, nor precious stones. The reason for the downfall of Tyre is pride linked to the desire for riches. There is no mention in Ezek. 28.11-19 of a serpent, disobedience in eating from a tree, or the cursing of the ground.

On closer inspection, the Ezekiel passage is closest in content to Gen. 3.22-24, which describes expulsion from Eden and the activity of the guardian cherub. There are no exact parallels with 3.1-21, and there is no mention of the garden of *Eden* in

3.1-21, but merely of a garden. This is interesting in the light of §7 above, where the view was outlined that 3.22-24 is a literary device to link the original stories of Genesis 2 and 3 and to remove Adam and Eve from the Garden of Eden. It is difficult to escape the conclusion that, in the formation of Gen. 3.1-24, a story similar to that in Ezek. 28.11-19 was used, even if it was only to provide a narrative unity for stories different from that in the Ezekiel passage.

9. Cain and Abel

4.1-16 has parallels with 3.1-21, and can be regarded as either from the same source as 3.1-21 (J) or as deliberately composed in order to refer back to 3.1-21. The most striking similarities are:

1. the divine questions to the wrongdoers (3.9 and 4.9)
2. the curses (3.17 and 4.11).

From the thematic viewpoint, the story in 4.1-16 expands the wrong-doing of the human race. In Genesis 3 the man and woman quarrel over their responsibility for their disobedience to God (3.11-12). In 4.1-8, the sons of the man and woman quarrel, and one kills the other.

The narrative contains certain difficulties. We are not told why God preferred Abel's offerings of livestock to Cain's offerings of the produce of the land. Was Cain trying to ignore the curse upon the land of Gen. 3.17? Another difficulty is that, according to 9.6, the penalty for murder is death, but Cain is spared that. It could be argued, from the order of events in the narrative of Genesis 1–11, that Cain is not subject to a law not yet promulgated. However, in v. 14 Cain says that he will be killed by anyone who finds him wandering on the earth. This can hardly be in revenge for the murder of his brother, since that duty would fall within the family of Abel, and not simply anyone whom Cain chanced to meet. This last theme raises, of course, two questions: from where would these people come who might slay Cain, given that only three humans exist (Adam, Eve and Cain if we read the narrative literally); and who will avenge Cain sevenfold if he is slain?

If these problems were recognized by Israelite readers or hearers of this material, they were probably not a cause for anxiety. Cain, like Adam and Eve, is a type, and he represents human beings who violate the closest bonds of kinship. The narrative expresses God's condemnation of such action, while at the same time containing hints of the dangers of living the itinerant life of metal workers, who are descended from Cain (vv. 17-22).

The most important passage in the story is that which describes how the shedding of innocent blood affects the fertility of the land (vv. 10-12). The created order is not a machine that functions regardless of the behaviour of human beings. As pointed out above (§5) there is a link between human morality and obedience to God, and the fertility of the land. Even crimes not noticed or detected by human beings are an affront to God, bringing punishment to the offenders and loss of strength to the earth. The passage expresses the conviction of Old Testament faith that to believe in creation is to believe in an order in which human relationships play their part. The action of Cain is, in effect, an undoing of creation. However, Genesis 4 ends with an important reference to God's graciousness at work in the midst of human evil. The birth of Seth (v. 25) sets up the line from which Noah will come, and people begin to call on the name of YHWH.

10. Long-lived patriarchs

Between the Cain and Abel narrative and that of the Flood there is a list of ancestors, whose function is to show how the world became populated. In Gen. 5.1-28, 30-32 we have what is ascribed by source criticism to the P source; and it is interesting that the list of ancestors has similarities with what is regarded as the J passage of 4.17-21. These can be shown as follows:

4.17-21	5.1-28, 30-32
[Adam]	Adam
	Seth
	Enosh
Cain	Kenan

Mehujael	Mahalalel
Irad	Jared
Enoch	Enoch
Methushael	Methuselah
Lamech	Lamech
Noah (5.29)	Noah

The order of the generations in 4.17-21 is different from that in 5.1-28, being Cain–Enoch–Irad–Mehujael–Methushael–Lamech, but the similarities are sufficiently strong to suggest (if one accepts source division) that J and P had access to similar traditions about the descendants of Adam to the time of Noah.

5.29 is assigned by source criticism to J because of its reference back to the cursing of the ground and the toil of labour (3.17; 4.12). The English translations are not always helpful for this verse, and the Hebrew verb rendered (in RSV) as 'bring...relief' strictly means 'comfort'.

If source division is correct, then 5.1 in the P source resumes from 2.4a, and P has no 'fall' story until it reaches 6.11. Striking are the great ages attained by the descendants of Adam, with Methuselah reaching the greatest age of all, 969 years. In this, Genesis 5 can be compared with the Sumerian king lists (*ANET*, pp. 265-66) according to which the kings who reigned before the Flood had much longer reigns than those who came after the Flood. Before the Flood, the first two kings reigned for 64,800 years, whereas after it twenty-three kings achieved only just over 24,510 years. The Genesis figures are modest by comparison, but they are sufficiently out of line with normal human expectations to make the point that the people who lived before the Flood lived in an age which is no longer accessible.

The case of Enoch, who did not die but was 'taken' by God because of his close relationship with God (5.24) is an expression in the Old Testament of the view that fellowship with God cannot be broken by death. However, this is very much a minority theme in the Old Testament.

11. Gods, women and giants

Genesis 6.1-4 is a strange and fascinating passage. In one sense, it adds nothing to the overall narrative since, if there are sources, 6.5 (J) refers back to 4.24 as the reason for the Flood while P gives its reason for the Flood at 6.11. On a 'final form' reading the passage connects with the very long lives of the ancestors, and reduces the life-span of humans to 120 years as a punishment either for the inter-marriage of the 'sons of God' and the daughters of man or for the wickedness described in ch. 4. However, as is clear from 11.10ff., the descendants of Noah lived to be well over 120 years (Shem lived for 600 years according to 11.10-11) although their longevity gradually declined as the generations descended towards the time of Abraham. A good case can be made for seeing 6.1-4 as a tradition that was added quite late to the composition as a whole, not only on account of its awkwardness in its context and its contradiction of other material, but on linguistic grounds (the Hebrew phrase rendered 'for'—$b^e\check{s}aggam$—looks like later Hebrew). Scholars disagree as to whether the 'sons of God' are divine beings who marry human women, or are mighty rulers who arbitrarily take women for their harem (cf. the end of 6.2). On the face of it, the explanation that 'sons of God' means mighty rulers is less obvious than taking 'sons of God' at face value to mean divine beings. But in that case, why should God punish humankind in v. 3 for acts committed by divine beings?

Against the background of ancient literature it can be noted that the increase in human population is the prelude to the Flood in the *Atra-hasis* story (Lambert and Millard, p. 73). We may also notice that in the context of the idea of creation as order, 6.1-4 implies a confusion of boundaries, with divine beings and possibly giants inter-marrying with human beings.

If Gen. 6.1-4 is puzzling in its present context, it became the basis of much speculation in later interpretation. From it developed the idea of the fall of angels who lusted after the daughters of men, and thus the passage provided a basis for the dualistic understanding of the world that we find in inter-testamental Judaism and in Christianity.

12. One Flood story or two?

The source division of Genesis 1–11 into J and P is fairly
straightforward in chs. 1–5. But from 6.5 to 9.28, the source
theory entails that two independent stories of the Flood have
been woven together to form a single narrative. It is also supposed that it is possible to reconstruct these sources. This section will outline the reasons for the division into two sources,
and will point to some difficulties which it involves.

The strongest argument for the existence of two sources is
the presence of repetitions ('doublets'), and of distinctive verbs
and divine names.

1. 6.5-8 is parallel to 6.11-13 in subject matter. In the case of
   the former, the divine name is YHWH (LORD) while in the
   latter it is *ᵉlōhîm* (God). Also, the verb 'blot out' is used in
   v. 7 (Heb. *māḥâ*) whereas 'destroy' (Heb. *hšmd*) is used in
   v. 13.
2. 7.1-5 is parallel to 6.19-22, and the passages have the
   divine names YHWH (LORD) and *ᵉlōhîm* (God) respectively.
   In 7.1-5 Noah is instructed to take into the ark seven pairs
   of clean and one pair of unclean animals, but in 6.19-22 he
   is to take pairs of everything.
3. 7.7-10 is parallel to 7.13-15. Both passages relate an entry
   into the ark.
4. 7.22-23 is parallel to 7.18-21. 7.21 says that all creatures
   remaining on earth died, a sentiment immediately
   repeated by 7.22. 7.23 reads, 'He blotted out every living
   thing', but there is no close antecedent for the 'he', which
   suggests that this passage has been taken from a source in
   which there was an antecedent.

On the basis of these, and other, considerations, it can be suggested that the following passages belonged to the separate
sources:

J	P
6.5-8	
	6.9-21
7.1-5	
	7.6
7.7-10 (part)	
	7.11, 13-15, 18-21

7.22-23	
	7.24–8.5
8.6-12	
	8.13a, 14-19
8.20-22	
	9.1-17

Not all verses have been assigned to sources, as there are some uncertainties.

If we examine the proposed sources, we see that P is a more complete story than J. In J there is no command to build an ark, nor any account of Noah's leaving the ark after the Flood. On the other hand, the J passages link well together, especially 8.20-22 which looks back to 6.5-8. Both passages mention the evil imagination of the human heart, while the reference to not cursing the ground again (8.21) is reminiscent of 5.29, 4.11 and 3.17 (all of which are verses ascribed to J), although 8.21 uses a different Hebrew verb from that in the other passages.

If the narrative was compiled from two sources there are two views as to how this was done. According to one view, the P writer incorporated the J material into his narrative. According to the other view, a later redactor combined P and J, using P as the main narrative.

Against the source division theory, it can be asked why P, or a redactor, should have left the parallel passages, detailed above, side by side, while presumably eliminating the J versions of the manufacture of the ark and Noah's exit from it after the Flood. A partial answer can be given in that 6.5-8 and 8.20-22 provide an artistic beginning and end to the story, and the retention of 6.5-8 then produces a parallel with 6.11-13. On the other hand, it is difficult to explain why P or the redactor should have retained the parallel and contradictory accounts of the entry into the ark. There is a further problem in that one of the J passages (7.7-10) has the 'wrong' divine name and does not discriminate between clean and unclean animals as it is supposed that J does. If 7.7-10 has been edited by a redactor in order to make it conform to the P account, as is often supposed, then why did this editor do such a minimal job of trying to remove the inconsistencies?

It is often urged against the source division that we have no evidence from the ancient world that authors combined separate narratives together. This, however, has recently been contested by Tigay (Tigay, 1985). The evidence of Tigay does not prove the source division theory in the case of the Flood, but removes the argument that the use of sources is supported by no examples from the ancient world. That the case for sources in Gen. 6.5–9.17 is not absolutely conclusive is indicated by the continuing discussion of the matter (see the literature in the Bibliography).

13. Noah's drunkenness and Canaan's curse

9.20-27 contains an obvious difficulty. Why is it that Noah curses not Ham, whose wrongdoing is described in v. 22, but Ham's son Canaan (v. 25)? The probable answer is that in 9.20-27 two originally separate traditions have been combined together. The first, in vv. 20-23, is similar to the tradition in 4.22. In the latter passage, Tubal-Cain is described as the (original) forger of bronze and iron implements. Here Noah is named as the first tiller of the soil, who planted a vineyard. In other stories set in beginning time, there is mention of the founders of institutions known to the readers. It is interesting that in the case of Noah, his extension of the benefits of civilization is not an unqualified success. It leads to drunkenness, and to his being naked in his tent. The offence of Ham was not so much that he saw his father naked, but that, unlike his brothers, he did nothing to remedy his father's disgrace. The whole passage indicates that the family from which the whole human race is to descend is capable of actions that are not worthy of humanity at its best.

The poem of 9.25-27 is similar to the curses that have preceded it in Genesis, as well as being similar to the blessings and curses given by the patriarch Isaac (27.23-29, 39-40) and Jacob (49.3-27). These pronouncements reflect political circumstances known to the readers, and invest these circumstances with a sanctity derived from the reputation of the speaker of the blessings and curses. That 9.25-27 is an ancient poem is probably indicated by its obscurities. Verse 25 is comparatively straightforward. The cursing of Canaan in terms of condemning him to slavery no doubt reflects the situation in the reigns of David and Solomon when the Canaanites were

subordinate to the Israelites. Verse 26 is less easy. On the face
of it, it means 'Blessed be the LORD, the God of Shem' (see RSV
footnote) but it makes no sense in a blessing of sons, hence the
RSV's text 'Blessed by the LORD my God be Shem' which
involves a slight revocalization of the Hebrew. Even this is
inane, and one wonders whether the text has been lost or
hopelessly corrupted.

The blessing of Japheth seems to retain the original text,
since there is a pun on the name Japheth and on the verbal
form translated 'enlarge' (*yepet* and *yapt*). It is difficult,
however, to know what it means when the text says 'let him
dwell in the tents of Shem'. On the face of it, this implies a dis-
placement of Shem by Japheth, but this is difficult because
Shem is the ancestor of the Hebrews and Japheth is the
ancestor of sea-going peoples and islanders. The commonly
accepted explanation that the verse refers to the employment
of foreigners at the court of David or Solomon is not obvious.
We have to say that we do not know what this verse meant
either 'originally' or to readers in context. What is clear is that,
generally speaking, 9.20-27 taken together functioned to show
that the human race after the flood was not perfect, and that
the subjugation of the Canaanites by the Israelites was a punishment ordained by the principal human survivor of the flood.

14. The genealogies (Genesis 10)

According to source division, Genesis 10 is composed of two
types of narrative. The P narrative is characterized by a formulaic mode of expression (10.1a, 2-7, 20-23, 31-32): 'The sons
of n: a, b, c...The sons of a: d, e, f, etc.', concluding with 'these
are the sons of n with their families, language(s), lands'. The J
material (10.1b, 8-19, 21, 24-30) is much more of a narrative
with various anecdotes about individuals and nations. Even if
readers do not accept the source theory, they must notice that
we have two types of material juxtaposed: the formulaic and
the narratival/anecdotal.

These two types of material perform two functions. The
formulaic material indicates how the descendants of Noah
spread all over the earth, in fulfilment of the command of 9.1
to 'be fruitful and multiply, and fill the earth'. The narrative/

anecdotal material informs Israelite readers about the origins of peoples familiar to them either from their reading of Genesis as a whole, or from their knowledge of the ancient world. Thus, among the places and peoples mentioned in 10.10-14, the names Babel (Babylon), Nineveh, Egypt and Philistines occur, while in 10.15-19 the significant names include Canaan, Sidon, the Jebusites, Gerar, Gaza, Sodom, Gomorrah, Admah and Zeboim. Well-known names in 10.25-29 are Sheba, Ophir and Havilah.

The narratival/anecdotal material is reminiscent of 4.17-22, where Jabal is the father of those who dwell in tents and have cattle, and Tubal-cain is the (original) forger of metal instruments (4.20, 22). In 10.8, Nimrod is the first on earth to be a mighty man—a statement that appears to contradict 6.4 which mentions mighty men before the flood.

A possible key verse for the understanding of the chapter is v. 9, where Nimrod is described as a 'mighty hunter before the LORD'. Nimrod is apparently unknown elsewhere in ancient literature, although the present passage generated many traditions about him in later Jewish and Islamic writings. If, as seems most likely, the verse is taken to be a compliment to Nimrod, then we have a non-Israelite described both as a founder of civilization in Babylon and Assyria, and as standing in some sort of relationship to God. From this we could conclude that the chapter is saying that not only did the nations consist of men and women created by the God worshipped by Israel, but that among these nations were individuals who enjoyed the favour of the God worshipped by Israel. We must not overlook the fact that the Old Testament has a strong sense that foreign nations can be used by God (cf. Isa. 10.5; 45.1), and that God's purpose in calling Abraham is to bring blessing to all nations (Gen. 12.3).

The material that makes up Genesis 10 is a necessary narrative device to populate the world following the reduction of the human race to one family by means of the flood. However, in the process of describing the spread of the human race, the chapter makes the world more 'friendly' for Israelite readers by mentioning cities, countries and peoples familiar to them, and by implying that the knowledge of the God worshipped by Israel was not entirely missing among these peoples.

15. The Tower of Babel

Read in sequence, Genesis 10 and 11.1-9 appear to be contradictory. 11.1 says that the whole earth had one language, whereas 10.5, 20 and 31 imply that each nation had its own distinct language. Even if we invoke source criticism, and say that 11.1-9 comes from J while 10.5, 20 and 31 are 'P' passages, the difficulties are not entirely removed. 10.10 states that Nimrod ruled over Babylon (Babel) while 11.9 can be read to indicate that the destruction of the tower led to the founding of Babel.

It is quite possible that the writer or editor of Genesis 1–11 saw 11.1-9 as a flashback to a time early in the spread of the nations over the earth, and that the scattering described in 11.9 was then part of the process of the spread of the nations.

Within the overall structure of Genesis 1–12, ch. 11 sets up a contrast between the scattering of the people because of their desire to assert themselves apart from God, and the obedience of Abram in 12.1-3 which will be the basis for a blessing of the nations.

The story has some similarities with Genesis 3, not only in content but in language. In Genesis 3 the man and woman eat a fruit which will help them to become 'like God'. Here, the desire of the human beings seems to be to reach heaven, God's dwelling place (11.4). The theme of the violating of boundaries can be observed here, and as in Genesis 3 God addresses himself in the first person plural, and determines to prevent further action by the human beings.

> Behold, they are one people... and nothing that they propose to do will be impossible for them (11.6).
> Come, let us go down, and there confuse their language (11.7).

In Genesis 3 God expels the human beings from the garden; here he scatters the human race from the plain in the land of Shinar.

A closer reading of the story indicates one or two unevennesses. For example, in v. 7 God determines to confuse the people's languages, but in v. 8 he scatters them abroad. No doubt the act of scattering peoples will result in the development of different languages, but one wonders whether the biblical writer or his presumed readers knew about how languages develop. There is also the fact that twice God 'comes down' (vv. 5, 7) although on the second occasion this is expressed as a resolve to do so. Because of these unevennesses, it has been suggested that two stories have been woven together here, one dealing with the origin of languages (11.1-2, 6-7), the other concerning an attempt to build a city, which God frustrated (11.3-5, 8). The explanation for the name of Babel would, on this view, have been added after the two stories were joined. Whether or not this is convincing, it draws attention to elements in the text.

An interesting question is whether there is any basis in fact to the story. It has good local colouring, in that building in Babylon was done in bricks baked from clay, whereas in Judah and Israel there was an abundance of stone for building. One candidate for an unfinished building that might have inspired the story is the Etemenanki Temple in Babylon, begun in the reign of Nebuchadnezzar I (1123–1101 BCE) and apparently not completed for many centuries (von Soden 1985, pp. 134-47).

16. The date of Genesis 1–11

This question has been left until last partly because it is difficult to settle, and partly because it can distract readers from looking at the text closely. The simple answer to the question of date is that Genesis 1–11 is part of the larger work containing Genesis to 2 Kings (minus Ruth which appears elsewhere in the Hebrew order of books of the Bible). This complete work did not reach its final form until during or after the Babylonian exile in the sixth century BCE. However, the date of the final editing does not determine the date of the individual items to be found in Genesis 1–11.

If one accepts the source theory, there are two possibilities. Most source critics would agree that P^g was composed during the exilic or post-exilic periods; and if the writer of P^g used older materials, it is impossible to determine their age. On the date of J there is a majority view that places it in the period of the Israelite monarchy, possibly as early as the reign of

Solomon. A growing minority view, however, is that J was composed during the exilic or post-exilic periods.

The arguments about the dating of J are circumstantial and not conclusive. As far as Genesis 1–11 is concerned, we saw in Chapter 2 that Wittenberg assumes a Solomonic date for J because he believes that he can detect in Genesis 3 and 11 a critique of royal building activities and the attempt of the king to assume wisdom that is appropriate only to God.

However, it is possible to argue in quite a different way. For example, if it is maintained that part of Genesis 3 is dependent upon Ezek. 28.11-19, then Genesis 3 must be dated to the exile at the earliest, since the Ezekiel passage is to be placed in the first half of the sixth century. Again, the story of the Tower of Babel can be said to fit best into the period when the Israelites were in exile in Babylon. In that case, the story would be a condemnation of the greatness of Babylon, and a declaration of its nothingness compared with the might of the God of Israel.

Attempts to date elements of Genesis 1–11 are at best plausible rather than probable, and involve circular arguments. This is not to say that it is wrong to try to date parts of Genesis 1–11, but rather that we should not allow such attempts to make us read the text superficially, as though we knew all that it has to say once we have assigned a date and setting. Even if we could be certain about dates and settings, we should still have to consider the following questions: how do the narratives function within the whole, and what interest do we, the readers, bring with us to the interpretation of Genesis 1–11?

Further Reading

1. *Works referred to in the text*
Anderson, B.W. (ed.)
    1984   *Creation in the Old Testament*. London: SPCK.
Beauchamp, P.
    1987   'Création et fondation de la loi en Gn 1,1–2,4', in F. Blanquart (ed.), *La Création dans l'orient ancien*. Paris: Les Éditions du Cerf, 139-82.
Bentzen, A.
    1970   *King and Messiah*. Oxford: Basil Blackwell.

Bird, P.A.
    1981   ' "Male and Female He Created Them": Gen. 1.27b in the Context of the Priestly Account of Creation', *HTR* 74, 129-59.

Brett, M.G.
    1990   'Motives and Intentions in Genesis 1' (forthcoming in *JTS*).

Calvin, John
    1965   *Genesis* (trans. by John King). Edinburgh: Banner of Truth Trust (reprint of 1874 edition).

Childs, B.S.
    1979   *Introduction to the Old Testament as Scripture.* London: SCM.

Clines, D.J.A.
    1978   *The Theme of the Pentateuch* (JSOTS 10). Sheffield: JSOT Press.

Collins, A.Y.
    1985   *Feminist Perspectives on Biblical Scholarship* (SBL Centennial Publications 10). Chico: Scholars Press.

Delano, J.H.
    1989   *The 'Exegesis' of 'Enuma Elish' and Genesis 1—1875 to 1975: A Study in Interpretation* (PhD Marquette University). Ann Arbor: University Microfilms.

Delitzsch, Friedrich
    1903   *Babel and Bible.* London: Williams and Norgate.

Fiorenza, E.S.
    1985   'Remembering the Past in Creating the Future: Historical-Critical Scholarship and Feminist Interpretation', in Collins, *Feminist Perspectives*, 43-63.

Jobling, D.
    1980   'The Myth Semantics of Genesis 2.4b–3.24', *Semeia* 18, 41-49.

Lambert, W.G. and A.R. Millard.
    1969   *Atra-Ḫasis. The Babylonian Story of the Flood.* Oxford: Clarendon.

Lohfink, N.
    1977   *Unsere grossen Wörter. Das Alte Testament zu Themen dieser Jahre.* Freiburg im Breisgau: Herder. (English translation by R. Walls, *Great Themes from the Old Testament.* Edinburgh: T. & T. Clark, 1982.)
    1983   'Die Schichten des Pentateuch und der Krieg', in N. Lohfink (ed.), *Gewalt und Gewaltlosigkeit im Alten Testament* (Quaestiones Disputatae 96). Freiburg im Breisgau: Herder.

Meyers, C.
    1988   *Discovering Eve. Ancient Israelite Women in Context.* New York: Oxford University Press.

Müller, H.-P.
    1972   'Mythische Elemente in der jahwistischen Schöpfungserzählung', *ZTK* 69, 259-89.
    1985 'Das Motif für die Sintflut. Die hermeneutische Funktion des Mythos und seiner Analyse', *ZAW* 97, 295-316.

Patte, D. (ed.)
    1980   Genesis 2 and 3. Kaleidoscopic Structural Readings. (*Semeia* 18).

Rad, G. von
1936   'The Theological Problem of the Old Testament Doctrine of Creation', in B.W. Anderson (ed.), *Creation in the Old Testament*, 53-64.
Rogerson, J.W.
1974   *Myth in Old Testament Interpretation* (BZAW 134). Berlin: de Gruyter.
1978   *Anthropology and the Old Testament*. Oxford: Basil Blackwell (reprint 1984; Sheffield: JSOT Press).
1980   'Herders Bückeburger "Bekehrung"', *Bückeburger Gespräche über Johann Gottfried Herder 1979*. Rinteln: C. Bösendahl, 17-30.
1984   *Old Testament Criticism in the Nineteenth Century: England and Germany*. London: SPCK.
1988   'The Old Testament', in J. Rogerson, C. Rowland, B. Lindars, *The Study and Use of the Bible*. Basingstoke: Marshall Pickering, 1-150.
1989   'Anthropology and the Old Testament' in R.E. Clements (ed.), *The World of Ancient Israel. Sociological, Anthropological and Political Perspectives*. Cambridge: Cambridge University Press, 17-37.
Rogerson, J.W. and P.R. Davies
1989   *The Old Testament World*. Cambridge: Cambridge University Press; Englewood Cliffs: Prentice Hall.
Schmid, H.H.
1973   'Creation, Righteousness, and Salvation: "Creation Theology" as the Broad Horizon of Biblical Theology', in Anderson, *Creation in the Old Testament*, 102-17.
Schmidt, W.H.
1967[2] *Die Schöpfungsgeschichte der Priesterschrift. Zur Überlieferungsgeschichte von Genesis 1,1–2,4a und 2,4b–3,24* (WMANT 17). Neukirchen-Vluyn: Neukirchener Verlag.
Schottroff, L.
1988   'Die Schöpfungsgeschichte Gen 1,1–2,4a', in L. and W. Schottroff, *Die Macht der Auferstehung, sozialgeschichtliche Bibelauslegungen*. Munich: Kaiser.
Schottroff, W.
1983   'Arbeit und sozialer Konflikt im nachexilischen Juda', in L. Schottroff and W. Schottroff (eds.), *Mitarbeiter der Schöpfung. Bibel und Arbeitswelt*. Munich: Kaiser, 104-48.
Soden, W. von
1985   'Etemenanki vor Asarhaddon nach der Erzählung vom Turmbau zu Babel und dem Erra-Mythos', in H.-P. Müller (ed.), *Bibel und Alter Orient. Altorientalische Beiträge zum Alten Testament* (BZAW 162). Berlin: de Gruyter, 134-47.
Steck, O.H.
1975   *Der Schöpfungsbericht der Priesterschrift* (FRLANT 115). Göttingen: Vandenhoeck & Ruprecht.

Tigay, J.H.
	1985	'The Evolution of the Pentateuchal Narratives in the Light of the
			Evolution of the *Gilgamesh Epic'*, in J.H. Tigay (ed.), *Empirical
			Models for Biblical Criticism*. Philadelphia: University of
			Pennsylvania Press, 21-52.
Trible, P.
	1978	*God and the Rhetoric of Sexuality* (Overtures to Biblical Theology
			2). Philadelphia: Fortress.
Van Dyck, P.J.
	1990	'The Function of So-Called Etiological Elements in Narratives',
			ZAW 102, 19-33.
Wittenberg, G.H.
	1988	*King Solomon and the Theologians*. Pietermaritzburg: University
			of Natal Press.
West, G.
	1990	'Reading "The Text" and Reading "Behind the Text". The "Cain
			and Abel" Story in a Context of Liberation', in D.J.A. Clines *et al.*
			(eds.), *The Bible in Three Dimensions. Essays in Celebration of
			Forty Years of Biblical Studies in the University of Sheffield* (JSOTS
			87). Sheffield: JSOT Press. 279-99.
Zenger, E.
	1983	*Gottes Bogen in den Wolken. Untersuchungen zu Komposition und
			Theologie der priesterschriftlichen Urgeschichte* (Stuttgarter
			Bibelstudien 112). Stuttgart: Katholisches Bibelwerk.

Selected Bibliography

Recent Commentaries on Genesis 1–11
Brueggemann, W.
	1982	*Genesis* (Interpretation: A Bible Commentary for Preaching and
			Teaching). Atlanta: John Knox Press.
Gibson, J.C.L.
	1981	*Genesis*, vol. 1 (The Daily Study Bible). Edinburgh: St Andrews
			Press.
Scharbert, J.
	1983	*Genesis 1–11* (Die neue Echter Bibel). Würzburg: Echter.
Vawter, B.
	1977	*On Genesis: A New Reading*. London: Geoffrey Chapman; New
			York: Doubleday.
Wenham, G.J.
	1987	*Genesis 1–15* (Word Biblical Commentary 1). Waco: Word Books.
Westermann, C.
	1984	*Genesis 1–11: A Commentary* (trans. by J.J. Scullion). London:
			SPCK.

Source Criticism and Form-Criticism
Coats, G.W.
	1983	*Genesis with an Introduction to Narrative Literature* (The Forms
			of Old Testament Literature 1). Grand Rapids: Eerdmans.

Larsson, G.
1985   'The Documentary Hypothesis and the Chronological Structure of the Old Testament', *ZAW* 97, 316-33.
Wenham, G.J.
1988   'Genesis: An Authorship Study and Current Pentateuchal Criticism', *JSOT* 42, 3-18.

see also Wenham, *Genesis 1-11*

Literary, Structuralist and Final Form Interpretations of Genesis 1-11
Anderson, B.W.
1978   'From Analysis to Synthesis. The Interpretation of Genesis 1-11', *JBL* 97, 23-39.
Carroll, M.P.
1977   'Genesis Restructured', in B. Lang (ed.), *Anthropological Approaches to the Old Testament*, London: SPCK, 127-35.
Gros Louis, K.R.R.
1974   'The Garden of Eden', in K.R.R. Gros Louis (ed.), *Literary Interpretation of Biblical Narratives*, vol. 1. Nashville, 41-58.
Hauser, A.J.
1982   'Genesis 2-3: The Theme of Intimacy and Alienation', in D.J.A. Clines *et al.* (ed.), *Art and Meaning: Rhetoric in Biblical Literature* (JSOTS 19). Sheffield: JSOT Press, 20-36.
Jobling, D.
1986   'Myth and its Limits in Gen. 2.4b–3.24', in D. Jobling, *The Sense of Biblical Narrative. II. Structural Analyses in the Hebrew Bible* (JSOTS 39). Sheffield: JSOT Press.
Wolde, E.J. van
1989   *A Semiotic Analysis of Genesis 2-3. A Semiotic Theory and Method of Analysis Applied to the Story of the Garden of Eden* (Studia Semitica Neerlandica 25). Assen: van Gorcum.

Liberation interpretations of Genesis 1-11
Crüsemann, F.
1980   'Autonomie und Sünde. Gen 4,7 und die "jahwistische" Urgeschichte', in W. Schottroff and W. Stegemann (eds.), *Traditionen der Befreiung. 1. Methodische Zugänge*. Munich: Kaiser, 60-77.
Link, C.
1986   'Der Mensch als Schöpfer und als Geschöpf', in J. Moltmann (ed.), *Versöhnung mit der Natur?* Munich: Kaiser, 15-47.
Boesak, A.
1989   *Black and Reformed: Apartheid, Liberation and the Calvinist Tradition*. Johannesburg: Skotaville, 148-57.

See also Wyatt, 'Interpreting the Creation...'

Feminist Interpretations of Genesis 1-11 and Women's Questions
Tischler, N.M.
1977   *Legacy of Eve. Women of the Bible*. Atlanta: John Knox. (Chapter 1: 'Eve–The Complete Woman'.)
Schelkle, K.H.
1977   *Der Geist und die Braut. Die Frau in der Bibel*. Düsseldorf: Patmos. (Chapter 1: 'Schöpfung und Schuld'.)

Laffey, A.L.
1988   *An Introduction to the Old Testament. A Feminist Perspective.*
        Philadelphia: Fortress.

Myth
Müller, H.-P.
1983   'Mythos—Anpassung—Wahrheit. Vom Recht mythischer Rede
        und deren Aufhebung', *ZTK* 80, 1-25.
Rogerson, J.W.
1990   'Myth', in R.J. Coggins and J.L. Houlden (eds.), *A Dictionary of
        Biblical Interpretation*, London: SCM, 479-82.

Ecological Interpretations of Genesis 1–11
Anderson, B.W.
1984   'Creation and Ecology', in B.W. Anderson (ed.), *Creation in the Old
        Testament*, London: SPCK, 152-78.

Genesis 1–11 and Ancient Near Eastern and Greek Literature
Cunchillos, J.-L.
1987   'Peut-on parler de mythes de création à Ugarit?', in F. Blanquart,
        La Création dans l'orient ancien, 79-96.
Jacobsen, T.
1981   'The Eridu Genesis', *JBL* 100, 513-29.
Oden, R.A., Jr
1981   'Divine Aspirations in Atrahasis and in Genesis 1–11', *ZAW* 93,
        197-216.
Pettinato, G.
1971   *Das altorientalische Menschenbild und die sumerischen und
        akkadischen Schöpfungsmythen* (Abhandlungen der Heidelberger
        Akademie der Wissenschaften. Phil.-Hist. Klasse 1). Heidelberg:
        Heidelberger Akademie der Wissenschaften.
Seux, M.-J.
1987   'La Création du monde et de l'homme dans la littérature suméro-
        akkadienne', in F. Blanquart (ed.), *La Création dans l'orient
        ancien*, 41-78.
Shea, W.H.
1984   'A Comparison of Narrative Elements in Ancient Mesopotamian
        Creation-Flood Stories with Genesis 1–9', *Origins* 11, 9-29.
Van Seters, J.
1988   'The Primeval Histories of Greece and Israel Compared', *ZAW*
        100, 1-22.

See also Bryan, 'A Reevaluation of Gen. 4 and 5 . . .'

Genesis 1
Jónsson, G.A.
1988   *The Image of God. Genesis 1.26-28 in a Century of Old Testament
        Research* (Coniectanea Biblica, OT series 26). Stockholm: Almqvist
        & Wiksell.

Genesis 2–3
Burns, D.E.
    1987   'Dream Form in Genesis 2.4b–3.24: Asleep in the Garden', *JSOT* 37, 3-14.
Day, J.
    1990   'Creation Narratives', in R.J. Coggins and J.L. Houlden (eds.), *A Dictionary of Biblical Interpretation*, London: SCM, 147-50.
Dockx, S.
    1981   *Le Récit du paradis. Gen. 2–3*, Paris-Gembloux: Duculot.
Joines, K.R.
    1975   'The Serpent in Gen. 3', *ZAW* 87, 1-11.
Moberly, R.W.L.
    1988   'Did the Serpent Get it Right?', *JTS* ns 39, 1-27.
Steck, O.H.
    1970   *Die Paradieserzählung. Eine Auslegung von Genesis 2,4b–3,24* (Biblische Studien 60). Neukirchen-Vluyn: Neukirchener Verlag.
Wyatt, N.
    1981   'Interpreting the Creation and Fall Story in Genesis 2–3', *ZAW* 93, 10-21.

Genesis 4–5
Bryan, D.T.
    1987   'A Reevaluation of Gen. 4 and 5 in Light of Recent Studies in Genealogical Fluidity', *ZAW*, 180-88.
Davies, P.R.
    1986   'The Sons of Cain', in J.D. Martin and P.R. Davies (eds.), *A Word in Season: Essays in Honour of William McKane* (JSOTS 42). Sheffield: JSOT Press 35-56.

See also Crüsemann, 'Autonomie und Sunde'

Genesis 6–8
Volkmar, F.
    1982   '"Solange die Erde steht"—Vom Sinn der jahwistischen Fluterzählung in Gen. 6–8', *ZAW*, 599-614.
Wenham, G.J.
    1978   'The Coherence of the Flood Narrative', *VT* 28, 336-48.

Genesis 10
Oded, B.
    1986   'The Table of Nations (Genesis 10)—A Socio-Cultural Approach', *ZAW* 98, 14-31.

INDEXES

INDEX OF BIBLICAL REFERENCES

INDEX OF AUTHORS